Adobe Days

LLEWELLYN BIXBY AND SARAH HATHAWAY
Their wedding picture

ADOBE DAYS

BEING

THE TRUTHFUL NARRATIVE of the Events in the Life
of a California Girl on a Sheep Ranch and in El Pueblo
de Nuestra Señora de Los Angeles While It Was
Yet a Small and Humble Town;

TOGETHER WITH

AN ACCOUNT of How Three Young Men from
Maine in 1853 Drove Sheep & Cattle Across
The Plains, Mountains, & Deserts from
Illinois to the Pacific Coast;

AND

THE STRANGE Prophecy of Admiral Thatcher
About San Pedro Harbor

By SARAH BIXBY SMITH
Introduction *by* ROBERT ERNEST COWAN

Foreword by Gloria Ricci Lothrop

University of Nebraska Press
Lincoln and London

First Bison Book Printing: 1987
Most recent printing indicated by the first digit below:
2 3 4 5 6 7 8 9 10

Library of Congress Cataloging-in-Publication Data
Bixby Smith, Sarah, 1871–1935.
Adobe Days
Reprint. Originally published: 3rd ed. rev.
Los Angeles, Calif.: J. Zeitlin, 1931.
With new foreword.
''Bison book''—T.p. verso.
Includes Index.
1. Bixby Smith, Sarah, 1871–1935—Childhood and
youth. 2. Sheep ranches—California. 3. Frontier
and pioneer life—California—Los Angeles.
4. Los Angeles (Calif.)—Biography. I. Title.
F869.L853B583   1987   979.4'94   87-5936
ISBN 0-8032-4177-1
ISBN 0-8032-9178-7 (pbk.)

Reprinted from the Revised Third Edition published by
Jake Zeitlin, Los Angeles, in 1931.

The Rancho Los Cerritos Historic Site kindly provided
copies of the original photographs for use
in producing this reprint.

∞

TO MY FATHER

LLEWELLYN BIXBY

BORN IN NORRIDGEWOCK, MAINE, OCTOBER 4, 1825

ARRIVED IN SAN FRANCISCO, JULY 7, 1851

DIED IN LOS ANGELES, DECEMBER 5, 1896

F O R E W O R D

By Gloria Ricci Lothrop

Adobe Days by Sarah Bixby Smith provides a description of California between the mining rush and the tourist rush. It offers rare glimpses of early sheepherding at the San Justo Ranch in Monterey County and of daily life at Rancho Los Cerritos and Rancho Los Alamitos in today's Orange County. It also tells of life in Los Angeles in an era when both the author and the town were growing up. It was a time of change when the imaginative young Sarah marveled to see "barley fields sprout houses" and Willmore City rise on her favorite seaside strand.

This reminiscence takes us back to the green-shuttered communal dwelling at San Justo where the Bixby men, recently transplanted from Maine, introduced their new brides to life out west. It also takes us to ranches, once part of a vast Spanish land grant, which were home to Sarah in an era before there was a Long Beach, a Spruce Goose, or a hotel floating on the sea.

With an enviable recollection of detail and a poetic literary style, Sarah Bixby Smith transports the reader to those "halcyon, sun-lit days" when Los Angeles was not yet the nation's second largest city, nor the major point of foreign entry into the United States, but still "an infant prodigy of a town." The author leads us along her favorite city routes, the first in the nation to be illuminated by electric lights. Hanging from towering standards, these lights cast an unfamiliar incandescence, "A beautiful blue light" that could be seen through the windows of the Bixby homestead on Court Street. That world becomes the reader's world as Sarah's words trace the image of "bare brown velvet hills" bordering the ranches of Hollywood to the west. The vivid descriptions then lead the mind's eye eastward down a hillside, where a town is conjured, "a place of trees and cottages, of open spaces and encircling groves framed to the northeast by a ridge of blue mysterious mountains."

These recollections present a city "angelic in name only," however. Los Angeles in Sarah's youth was a dusty western town with many flat-roofed dwellings made of sun-dried bricks and roofed with pitch drawn from nearby pools of *brea,* or tar. The town had not yet overcome the fact that at a time when it claimed only twenty-four hundred citizens its murder rate was one per day.

The story of *Adobe Days* begins much earlier, at a time when "black, lean, longhorned cattle" still grazed on the sweeping acres of vast ranchos carved from recently secularized Franciscan mission lands. It begins with the surge of gold fever that impelled thousands of argonauts westward. Several Bixby brothers, as well as cousins—including Sarah's father, Llewellyn Bixby—responded to that lure and were sufficiently rewarded for their mining and mercantile efforts that they departed the settlement of Volcano with enough capital to purchase 1,800 sheep from various Illinois herders and to embark upon an uncommonly daring venture. They drove the sheep by way of Council Bluffs and the Great Salt Lake, later veering southwest and finally arriving with their herd in San Bernardino, California, on December 30, 1853. After resting some months in Pasadena, the enterprising herdsmen and their flock traveled northward to Rancho San Justo.

Flint, Bixby and Company—formed by Sarah's father, Llewellyn Bixby, in partnership with his cousins, Benjamin and Thomas Flint—became premiere along the woolgrowers in the state, who in 1850 claimed only 17,000 sheep and a wool clip of 5,500 pounds. A decade later California production, enhanced by the company's introduction of purebred Spanish Merino sheep, surpassed 2,600,000 pounds that sold for eighteen to thirty-five cents a pound.

Encouraged by increased profits during the Civil War, the company expanded, acquiring 110,000 acres in Southern California between 1864 and 1868. Rancho Los Cerritos, purchased in 1866, was described a few years later in the *Los Angeles Star* as "one of the most thoroughly and systematically managed sheep ranches in the county." Its efficiency was well rewarded as the price of wool soared to forty-five cents a pound. Reassured by the continued prosperity, a younger brother, John Bixby, subleased several thousand acres of Rancho Los Alamitos, acquiring it in 1883 in partnership with Flint, Bixby and Company and I. W. Hellman.

During these years Sarah Bixby Smith often visited the sheep ranches. She spent holidays at the sprawling acres that were once part of the rancho granted to Manuel Nieto in 1784. While visiting, young Sarah absorbed the details of pastoral life that enrich her account of childhood and adolescence in a recently settled region at the threshold of its own maturity.

Adobe Days, quoted extensively in a wide range of secondary sources, has appeared in several versions, the first being an abbreviated one entitled "A Little Girl in Old California," published in the *Annual*

Publications of the Historical Society of Southern California (1920, vol. 2, pt. 3). In 1923 the same publication (vol. 12, pt. 3) ran the "Diary of Dr. Thomas Flint: California to Maine and Return, 1851–55," which contained material that would be included in *Adobe Days*. Then, at the urging of family and friends, Sarah Bixby Smith expanded "A Little Girl in Old California," and the Torch Press of Cedar Rapids, Iowa, published it as *Adobe Days* in 1925. A second, revised edition was published the following year. When new material was made available by George H. Bixby and others, it was decided to publish 1,500 copies of an enhanced third edition in 1931. This edition was only the second publication by the respected bookman Jake Zeitlin, who assumed the task because *Adobe Days* "had some very fine personal recollections of growing up in Southern California as a member of the Bixby family." As a result of the publisher's subsequent corporate reorganization, a large number of unbound sheets from the book were turned over to Anderson and Ritchie Press, where they were inadvertently destroyed; the consequent scarcity enhanced interest in this edition. An additional paperback release of the text, along with Robert Cowan's introduction to the 1931 volume, was published in 1974 in honor of the fiftieth anniversary of the rare third edition.

Adobe Days, admired for both its authenticity and vitality, is frequently cited in other works. It is considered significant as a social record of a vanished era, even more so as a documentary record of the life of children and of women in late nineteenth-century California. It is equally valuable for the biographical insights it provides about the author herself. Each of these vantage points must be considered in assessing the historical significance of this respected remembrance of childhood.

First of all, the book's enduring popularity arises from the clear, closely detailed picture it provides of Southern California, especially Los Angeles, in the latter part of the nineteenth century. The town, grown beyond the confines of the pueblo, had by its hundredth year in 1881 not yet become a city. The booms had not yet transformed the groves and ranches into suburban town lots, and youthful Sarah Bixby could still lose herself at play amid stands "of yellow mustard ten feet tall." In well-remembered detail, she enumerates the native flowers that garlanded Bunker Hill, today a glistening corporate center but once only a languid moss-edged pond inhabited by sagacious frogs and even wiser fish that easily evaded Sarah's homemade hooks.

Her reminiscences include concerts featuring Adelina Patti during her several farewell tours, as well as the annual arrival of the Barnum and Bailey Circus. Sarah captures the excitement of both children and adults, roused by the appearance of the large white tent at Second and Spring streets. With engaging familial detail, she describes the historic reception for Mrs. Rutherford B. Hayes held at the St. Elmo Hotel, one of the growing number of caravansaries built by Los Angeles investers who boldly speculated that each economic boom was but a prelude to another.

It is within the well-seasoned walls of Rancho Los Cerritos, however, that the young Sarah's vision yields the most precious glimpse of vanished days. Passing through the large gate, she tours each room of the whitewashed adobe, sharing small remembrances and even smaller details of customs, tastes, and childish pranks; of shining pans of clotted cream in the milk room; of chocolate and brown sugar and gay boxes of Chinese tea, all suffused with the lingering aroma of dried apples, daily baked batches of doughnuts, and the aroma of the ubiquitous mutton stew.

Once Sarah is across the courtyard, the ranchers spring to life and she retraces their routine. With a calm born of familiarity, she describes the daily butchering of a sheep, and with contagious excitement she heralds the arrival of a dashing band of Mexican sheepshearers in "ruffled white shirts, high heeled boots and high-crowned, wide sombreros," astride their elegantly bedecked horses.

Despite the distracting bustle of ranch life, Sarah's seemingly all-encompassing gaze calmly follows the seasonal cycles of the native flora and traces the growth of the alien plants—the lilacs, roses, oleander, and verbena introduced by succeeding generations of immigrants to California. The procession of settlers created a cosmopolitanism still characteristic of the region today. This tradition of ethnic pluralism is implicitly acknowledged as Sarah Bixby Smith shares childhood memories of English, Irish and Portuguese ranch hands, Basque sheepherders, Chinese cooks, and a Jewish Rabbi who was the respected friend of her grandfather, a retired minister.

Unwittingly, perhaps, in her evocation of another era Sarah Bixby Smith has provided a rich resource in the study of Southern California's social history. Later works have substantially recorded the same period, notably Harris Newmark's *Sixty Years in Southern California, 1853–1913*, 4th ed. (Los Angeles: Zeitlin and Ver Brugge, 1970) and John Albert Wilson's *History of Los Angeles County, California* (Oakland, Calif.: Thompson and West, 1880; Berkeley, Calif.: Howell-North, 1959), but the views contained in *Adobe Days* provide the texture and suggest the actual quality of life in the region during the late nineteenth century.

Another facet of this narrative is its rare description of a child's life in the West, a topic infrequently considered, with the exception of John Baur's invaluable *Growing Up With California* (Los Angeles: Will Kramer, 1974). Although practitioners of the new social history, including Philippe Ariès and John Demos, have focused on children and the family, their pioneering efforts have thus far served only to underscore the important role of children in what essentially remains a silent history. Documents like *Adobe Days* must tell that story.

Initial research has suggested that, as a result of decreased infant mortality by the end of the nineteenth century, the detached and constrained attitudes of parents toward children were replaced by a new celebration of childhood as a clearly differentiated stage of life. This change is evidenced in the widespread observance of children's birthdays, the practice of writing baby biographies along the highly detailed outlines found in the popular baby books of the era, and in the general indulgence of infancy expressed in the growing acceptance of breast feeding, the use of unrestrictive infant clothing, and the encouragement of a wider range of sensory exploration by the child. The new prominence of the child within the social unit is implicit in the relationships described by Sarah Bixby Smith.

The latter part of the nineteenth century witnessed further changes in familial relationships as the mother was given increased responsibility for molding the child, now viewed more as a malleable and impressionable entity rather than as the earlier image of a creature of original sin. As a result, the American family became a more intimate and a more richly intense social environment—an environment in which the socializing of a generation of children assumed central importance. Since little documentation of these patterns exists, *Adobe Days* with its clearly drawn portrait of child life assumes particular significance. For example, parental response to the destruction of a newly purchased book, or to the igniting of an ill-advised fire on Christmas morning, underscores the importance placed on prompt discipline.

With the increasing acceptance of childhood as a social category and the decreasing importance of the family as a unit of economic production, childhood, no longer seen only as a preparation for later life, assumed a prima facie importance. Youthful play and recreation were accepted as ends in themselves. The pattern held for the heroine of *Adobe Days*, whose world was filled with dolls, games of marbles and jacks, and with glorious Fourth of July celebrations where, in addition to pin wheels and Roman candles, there were Chinese bombs, fire crackers, and torpedos safe enough for babies. Some play was work, like learning to sew patchwork, while actual work, like helping with the sheepshearing or gathering white goose feathers, was pursued with the exuberance of play. It is an exuberance the author repeatedly conveys, nowhere more than in her description of a trek through the black porridgelike mud of Los Angeles. Smith's description is a veritable paean to the forgotten childhood glories of mud.

Along with a new definition of childhood, the nineteenth century introduced a narrow definition of womanhood that led to increasingly rigid definitions of sexual roles. The resulting sexual segregation encouraged the development of specific female spheres, often marked by abiding same sex friendships. It is interesting that such a pattern is not alluded to by Sarah even in relation to her sister Anne, three years her junior. Instead, the narrative is filled with frequent references to adventures with cousins like Dick, with whom, during "her long sunny days of freedom with the boys," she made figure-four traps used to catch quail.

In her later childhood, this kinship with male relatives may have reflected Sarah's reaction to the loss of a significant role model after the death of her mother from typhus, a loss that she confesses she fully grasped only in later years. The additional deaths of a grandmother, uncles, and cousins also had an effect upon Sarah. Dolls died and were ceremonially interred, while the burial sites of animals and birds were carefully marked with headstones made of mud. Such childlike ways of coping with the inexplicable exigencies of death have been investigated by scholars of family history. Their contention that mortality within the family structure invariably initiates response from the survivors is amply illustrated in this unself-conscious account of youth growing to maturity.

One means of coping with the difficult period after a death in the family was to have children spend considerable time elsewhere, with the added purpose of fostering closer ties with an extended family network. Sarah's frequent sojourns at Rancho Los Cerritos represented such movement in and out of relatives' households. This pattern, particularly acceptable to the closely related Bixby men and Hathaway women, attributed to a permeable quality of family life and created for Sarah a changing, though reassuringly recognizable, tapestry of family ties.

Whether under her mother's tutelage or that of Aunt Martha, Sarah Bixby Smith's middle-class rearing reflected the common wisdom that, amid the array of expanding possibilities presented by the era, the young should be introduced to a coherent reality where values were clearly defined and virtue was extolled.

Convinced that literacy and restraint proceeded simultaneously, middle-class Americans of the era accorded great attention to the education of children. Thus, even amid the playful abandon at the rancho, Sundays were marked by regular church attendance at Gospel Swamp, followed by reading from appropriate literary classics or from the children's literature of the period. That literature presented reasonable and insistent moral choices while invariably advancing the preferability of industry, self-control, and deferred gratification. Sarah did not escape these injunctions, particularly in the course of mastering McGuffey's *Readers,* each chapter rich in homely invocations of national sentiment and civic virtue.

During her visits to the ranch, this pioneer schoolgirl could escape these more traditional patterns of socialization. Joining her father on long wagon rides through distant sheep pastures, she would be greeted by lonely Basque sheepherders who would welcome her with some small handcrafted toy of their creation. Ranch hands, sheepshearers, and itinerant peddlers were all part of her childhood panorama—by no means a world view, but one that provided variety to an otherwise insulated experience buffered by nannies, nurses, and Chinese cooks.

Central to the socialization of childhood is the peeling away of the protective layers of dependency. In the nineteenth century this ultimately led farm girls to seek employment in factory towns and more privileged young women to go away to school, as did Sarah, first to Oakland and Pomona and then to Wellesley, which offered the attendant cultural enrichments of the cosmopolitan center of Boston.

These excursions were formative experiences during the author's adolescence, although it is not clear whether the teenage years were then recognized as a separate phase of maturation. However, the literature does provide frequent allusions to "a period of brilliant and stormy crisis." There is also evidence that new work roles were assigned young girls in their middle years, not unlike the allocation of homemaking responsibilities to Sarah upon her return from school in Oakland. The family clearly perceived her approaching womanhood, and the prolonged absence of Aunt Martha provided ample opportunity for an apprenticeship in domesticity.

If the nineteenth century was the century of the child, it was also the century of the "cult of true womanhood." While childhood was being redefined, so was the female image. The model woman was ever more closely yoked to domesticity, dedicated to creating for her husband and children a stable refuge in an increasingly changing society. To help women succeed in this role of motherhood, abiding and ever virtuous, nineteenth-century books on manners and studies on pedagogy carefully circumscribed the realm of female experience.

A variant on this feminine model was found in the American West, however, where successful settlement depended upon the complementary labors of men and women. To the comparatively few

women settlers fell the additional tasks of maintaining the traditions of
the parent culture as well as establishing social institutions in the new
communities. As a result, women were encouraged to undertake civic
endeavors outside the home, and young girls were given freer access to
education. It is not surprising, therefore, that California granted women
the vote in 1911, nine years before the nation ratified the Nineteenth
Amendment.

Still another significant aspect of *Adobe Days* is that it provides
glimpses of woman's life during this period, particularly as it was lived
by those who ventured as far west as California. For example, the stalwart, self-reliant pioneer woman is epitomized by the newly married
Mary Johnson, who contributed to the "general comfort" of the Bixby
wagon train by baking bread and "on gala days making apple pies and
doughnuts." She was, at the same time, equally capable of wielding a
sharp hatchet against marauding Indians. Her successful completion of
the trip is particularly notable in view of the fact that she was delivered
of a son a scant two months after the group's arrival in California.

Adobe Days is replete with clues as to how life was lived within
women's sphere. These glimpses range from detailed wedding preparations to the women's communal domestic life at San Justo. The subsequent dispersal of these close neighbors suggests that the women may
have found uncomfortable the prolonged intimacy and the shared bur-
den of domestic responsibilities.

Sarah's own exposure to the life of a proper Victorian gentlewoman
was most emphatic during her sojourn at Field Seminary in Oakland,
where she was "allowed to walk alone around the corner [but] no street
was to be crossed." The regimen was a far cry from her carefree days at
Los Cerritos where, constrained only by a sunbonnet and a serviceable
pinafore, she and her cousin examined and explored with little evidence
of restraint. Perhaps it was such permissiveness, allowing girls the same
free range of investigation and exercise as boys, that encouraged the development of an independence and accomplishment among Bixby
women. Among them were Eulalia Bixby, one of the first Los Angeles
schoolteachers, and Dr. Mary Edmands, "an early physician in San
Francisco in the days when it took grit as well as brains for a woman to
gain a medical education," as proudly cited in *Adobe Days*.

Although this graceful backward glance at old California is in no way
an apologia or an indictment of the status of women at the time, the social history it conveys provides an important insight into a subject of
crucial interest to students of women's history in America.

Finally, this book is important for the information it provides about
the formative years of an important contributor to the development of

Southern California. Sarah Bixby Smith was a descendant "of seven passengers on that early emigrant ship, the *Mayflower*," a poet and a painter who was twice married, and the mother of five. She was an ardent advocate of history and a dedicated supporter of education and the arts. A leader in the women's club movement, she was undaunted by members' criticisms of her bold commitment to the peace movement.

Sarah Bixby Smith's abiding relationship to California was but briefly interrupted during her years at Wellesley and again shortly after her father's death in 1896 until 1904, during which time her husband's career took the couple to Michigan, to Hawaii, where he served for a year as president of Oahu Preparatory School, and thence to Massachusetts. In 1904 her husband secured a position in the philosophy department at Pomona College, where she had once studied, and the family settled in Claremont, a mere three blocks from Aunt Martha Hathaway, who had reared Sarah and her sister after their mother's untimely death. It was soon Sarah's opportunity to repay that kind nurturing by caring for her beloved but strong-willed aunt in the years before her death.

Sarah's life underwent a reordering as her marriage ended, her husband assuming a position as Unitarian minister at Berkeley, where soon after he married a former student. A similar position as substitute Unitarian minister in Pomona was later assumed by a Berkeley graduate student, Paul Jordan-Smith, who had arrived in California from Chicago in 1914 at the age of twenty-nine. The meeting of Sarah and Smith soon led to a marriage that enriched her life in many ways. To the Smiths' fourteen-room Claremont home, constructed of river rock and set amid twenty landscaped acres, came the literary figures of the era.

Paul Jordan-Smith, who produced four major books on Robert Burton, including the first all-English edition of Burton's *Anatomy of Melancholy* published in 1927, attracted visiting foreign literary figures like Rebecca West, as well as neighbors like Upton Sinclair and close friends like Charlie Chaplin, who once dropped in complaining of a malfunctioning Rolls Royce. To the delight of Sarah's two older boys, the comedian allowed them to tinker with the engine until it purred with renewed life. There were, as well, weekend getaways to Robinson Jeffers' Tor House near Carmel, and regular Saturday night dinners with Los Angeles book folk, highlighted by spaghetti, wine, and "a lot of good talk."

It was a rich and heady retinue of talent that made its way to the Claremont home, leading Jordan-Smith to observe that the mantel in the ample drawing room, if it could, might have recorded talk about drama, books and politics, about pacifism and war, and adding:

Over and over it would have recorded talk about Samuel Butler of Erewhon, Hardy of Max Gate, Anatole France of the Villa Said. And of those twentieth century writers I have read since 1932 the discussions were frequent concerning Macneile Dixon, Arnold Toynbee, Lucien Price, Alfred North Whitehead, Lin Yutang, George Templeton Strong, and that almost lost but very lively Captain Peter Drake, the Irish adventurer whose one book of "Memoirs" was suppressed as soon as it was issued — as long ago as 1755.

During those busy days, Sarah Bixby Smith filled numerous large canvasses with her sensitive interpretations. She also served on the local school board and as a trustee of Scripps College, one of the cluster of colleges that developed around Pomona College, organized in 1887 to promote "New England type education." From the outset, it had so impressed Sarah's grandfather, who had witnessed the school's first year-end exercise, that he urged her to join its fledgling student body in preparation for her later study at Wellesley.

When opportunity allowed, Sarah Bixby Smith would pack the children on the Santa Fe train to Los Angeles. Then, transferring to the Salt Lake line, they would proceed southward to Long Beach and her familiar rancho. At Christmas she would often arrive bearing hand-picked bouquets of wild flowers as tokens of the season and of her abiding affection for that world of childhood.

It was in her poetry, however, that she gave fullest expression to her feelings. Through verse, she articulated both her joy and personal sorrow, the reflective passages, as in "My Little Child," revealing the range of her mournful thoughts after the death of a son:

> Measured by the ages
> I know not wherein differ
> The short life and the long.
> (From *My Sagebrush Garden,* 1924)

Often the periods of poetry writing were interrupted by calls to action, as the Smiths assisted in the organization of the People's Council of America for Peace and Democracy. Their efforts culminated with a national convention in Chicago in 1917. In the process, the couple's political crusade became a source of irritation for the hired help as federal agents daily questioned cooks and maids, wanting to know if Germans were being entertained in the house.

Sarah, granddaughter of the Reverend George Whitefield Hathaway, whose home had been a way station on the underground railroad and

who stood among his ministerial colleagues in providing a platform
from which feminist and abolitionist Lucy Stone could deliver her
appeal, was as undaunted as her progenitor. She was frank in promoting
her ideas, no matter how controversial. Confiding to her son, Arthur
Maxon Smith, Jr., she confessed that she suddenly felt that she was
vegetating in Claremont. She had written her books and painted her pictures, she declared. Convinced that she was as good as the average person, she'd come into Los Angeles and prove it, having nothing else to
do.

True to her promise, Sarah Bixby Smith demonstrated her mettle in
1928, rising to the presidency of the respected Friday Morning Club,
established in the 1870s by Caroline Severance, who had also organized
the International Federation of Women's Clubs. Although Severance, a
former abolitionist and fervent suffragist, had encouraged independent
thought among the clubwomen, the group had over the decades become
more accustomed to expressions of conservative sentiment. As a result,
strong differences of opinion marked Sarah Bixby Smith's three years as
president.

Soon after the completion of her term of office, Smith completed *The
Bending Tree,* adding to her books of poetry, which by then included *My
Sagebrush Garden: A Book of California Verse* (Cedar Rapids, Iowa:
The Torch Press, 1924) and *Wind upon My Face* (Los Angeles: Jake
Zeitlin, 1929). She also joined the board of directors of the Historical
Society of Southern California, serving as second vice-president in
1935.

In the fall of that year, she and a companion contracted trichinosis
from tainted meat, which ultimately caused her death. During her illness
she seized the opportunity to share with her son her sound grasp of the
world around her, so clearly manifest in *Adobe Days,* by proposing a
careful transition in the family holdings.

It was this same practicality, infused with a love for the historic past,
that was acknowledged by the Historical Society of Southern California
after Sarah died on September 13, 1935. "Long remembered for her
friendly suggestions, ready wit and her cooperation . . . , she was pecu-
liarly fitted to develop the historical values incident to her wide experience and to preserve them in her written works."

In conclusion, it should be observed that, while Sarah Bixby Smith's
vibrant evocation is in praise of an era long past, the vitality of her state-
ment has generated a life of its own. It has also provided an added
dimension of life to those physical structures of her storied past, their
preservation and current use in part inspired by the visions and vignettes
captured in the pages of *Adobe Days.*

Rancho Los Cerritos, purchased by the second Llewellyn Bixby to prevent further deterioration, was in 1955 purchased by the City of Long Beach. In 1970 it was designated a National Historic Landmark and today serves as a museum, as does nearby Rancho Los Alamitos, which remained a working ranch operated by descendants of John Bixby until the site was deeded in 1970 to the city of Long Beach. The main house, containing a central portion constructed in 1806, as well as various farm buildings now concentrated within seven and a half acres, represent a museum of early rancho life. Although the land of San Justo Ranch is now in San Benito County instead of Monterey County, its sweeping vastness is still unspoiled. Twenty-four hundred acres are operated as a cattle ranch, while the house and remaining seventy-three acres serve as a spiritual retreat center administered by the Franciscan Order of Friars Minor.

Most importantly, the tale of the Bixby family in California lives on in the imagination of the readers. They may wish to trace further this family's adventures in Katherine Bixby Hotchkiss's *Christmas Eve at Rancho Los Alamitos* and *Trip with Father,* both published by the California Historical Society at San Francisco in 1971.

It is in *Adobe Days,* however, that the reader's imagination is most fully engaged as Sarah Bixby Smith leads us into her land of memory:

> Here I loiter, a child again.
> I smell the wild celery, still in its place
> And love the mustard's delicate lace
> Along the by-way, meandering free . . ."
> (From *My Sagebrush Garden*)

Contents

ILLUSTRATIONS

INTRODUCTION

CALIFORNIA is a land of contrasts, strongly and sharply defined. A long line of ocean-coast broken by only a few harbors of approach is arrayed against the towering snow-topped Sierra range. In the north the climate is cold and invigorating. In the south it is semi-tropical and languorous. Heavily timbered areas are features of the upper sections of the state. In the lower sections vegetation is scant and chiefly tropical. The wintry blasts and heavy snows of the northern forests are fairly met by the sirocco and burning heat of the southern deserts. In equal contrast was the population. In the north was the Nordic, busy, bustling, driving and purposeful. In the south were the Spanish and Mexican-Spanish, proud and independent, but whose activities were largely those of the siesta of today with its sueños of mañana. Four decades have wrought a wondrous change in the south. If it has not entirely been effected by Californians it at least has been in California.

Sarah Bixby Smith was born at the San Justo Ranch near the drowsy little village of San Juan Bautista. Her people were from Maine, and earlier had lived for several generations in Massachusetts. In 1849, a cousin of her father, Benjamin Flint, had joined the thousands who were on the way to California and the gold-diggings. Here he was followed by Sarah's father and other relatives in 1851. Among them was Benjamin's brother, Dr. Thomas Flint, whose narrative was recently published. From his journal and numerous letters she has supplied many historical details with accuracy and precision. In 1853, these men, three in all, organized the firm of Flint, Bixby & Company. Together with a few teamsters they made the long hazardous and dangerous overland journey from Illinois to San Gabriel in eight months. It was a very unusual undertaking for they drove before them a flock of more than 2000 sheep. Before they took final leave of civilization, they shrewdly sheared their flock and the amount of $1570 was the first reward that they received for their perilous enterprise. For grazing purposes the flock from time to time was driven upon various ranches in California until 1855, when they finally settled in Monterey County, on the San Justo Rancho. Here, many years later, the author, Sarah Bixby Smith, was born.

Domestic life in an adobe was varied and full of interest, and in *Adobe Days* the author has assembled the most minute details of life as it was in those halcyon, sun-lit days of yesterday. Minute as these details may be they are neither arid nor tiresome. The advantages and opportunities of the author were extensive and in this broad field her garner has been rich. Her years at San Justo were few, but much of her childhood and girlhood was passed in and near Los Angeles happily amidst adobe environments. Her descriptions of the life and activities of that town as it was before "big business" seized it are fascinating. The churches, theatres, markets, shops, Chinatown and the Mexican quarter, have all been portrayed clearly and colorfully.

There is upon the subject of California a vast extent of printed literature—several thousands of volumes by as many different authors all who have been inspired more or less by its history and romance. Of these Sarah Bixby Smith is one, but in her charming book there is one feature that is unique—child life in the California of yesterday. A few scant narratives may exist but they are the vague and uncertain recollections of age, hazy and faintly phosphorescent. In *Adobe Days*, they are brought out in strong relief and clearly drawn. The child of yesterday is the citizen of today and it were well to endow sociology with some definite accounts of the actual life and actions of childhood. Herein they are all graphically recorded. The sports, games and pastimes; manners crude and refined; customs, gentle and rude; misdemeanors and punishments; daily tasks and unappreciated "chores"; childish piety and juvenile paganism; polite performances and unholy activities; Sunday schools and day schools; rewards and merits; books and songs; joys and sorrows; comedy and pathos.

In her subtle way, Sarah Bixby Smith has disclosed the source of her strength, for naïvely she states that she read "McGuffey's Readers," as also did many thousands of others of us of her day and generation. That William H. McGuffey, LL.D. was king of the bromides is not contended, but his readers were easily the "First Sellers" of his time. Four millions of the last generation were nourished upon his pabulum, and though it was indeed predigested shredded wheat, many thousands have survived to contribute to the uplift in the general scheme of affairs. For us who read the fitful "Fourth" and the fatiguing "Fifth," there is a profound significance in the homely name of "McGuffey," even as Wordsworth wrote: "Thoughts that do often lie too deep for tears."

Adobe days have passed forever. The adobes have disappeared in decay or destruction, too often under the ruthless hand of progress. Even their former sites now obliterated are but faintly and sweetly reminiscent as were Goldsmith's memories of his beloved school at Auburn.

But if the adobes are gone we yet have the picture drawn by the competent and firm hand of Sarah Bixby Smith. A rare observation; a wide vision; a sense of humor, keen, whimsical and subtle; the mind of the historian; the eye of the artist; and the soul of the poet have all combined to endow us with a charming picture of the departed *Adobe Days* and life as they once were in the lotus land of Southern California.

ROBERT ERNEST COWAN.

FOREWORD

SE V E R A L years ago I wrote a short account of my childhood, calling it *A Little Girl of Old California*. At the suggestion of friends, I have expanded the material to make this book.

The recent discovery of diaries kept by Dr. Thomas Flint during two pioneer trips to this coast which he made in company with my father, and the generous permission to make use of them granted me by his sons, Mr. Thomas Flint and Mr. Richard Flint, have added much to the interest of the subject. I at first contemplated including them in this volume, but it has seemed wiser to publish them separately and they are now available through the publications of the Southern California Historical Society.

My information regarding the earlier history of the Cerritos Ranch was supplemented by data given me by my cousin, the late George H. Bixby.

The interesting letter predicting the development of the harbor at San Pedro, written by Admiral Henry Knox Thatcher to my grandfather, Rev. George W. Hathaway, is the gift of my aunt, Miss Martha Hathaway.

I wish here to express my gratitude to my husband, Paul Jordan Smith, and to my friend, Mrs. Hannah A. Davidson, for their constant encouragement to me during the preparation of *Adobe Days*.

SARAH BIXBY SMITH.

Claremont, California
October, 1925

NOTE TO SECOND EDITION

FOR certain suggestions and information which have been incorporated in this revised edition I wish to thank Mrs. Mary S. Gibson, Mrs. D. G. Stephens, Prof. Joseph Pijoan and Mr. Charles Francis Saunders.

S. B. S.

September, 1926

NOTE TO THIRD EDITION

DUE to the discovery of additional material much new matter is included in this edition. The book is informal and makes no attempt to be an exhaustive history, but every effort has been made to verify the accuracy of all statements.

For additional material incorporated in this edition of *Adobe Days* I thank Mr. Terry Stephenson, Mr. J. J. Mellus, Mr. A. L. Lovett, Mr. Thomas Flint, Dr. Edward Bixby, and Mr. George C. Flint.

S. B. S.

June, 1931

ADOBE DAYS

CHAPTER I

Background

I W A S born on a sheep ranch in California, the San Justo, near San Juan Bautista, an old mission town of the Spanish padres. It stands in the lovely San Benito Valley, over the hills from Monterey and about a hundred miles south of San Francisco.

The gold days were gone and the time of fruit and small farms had not yet come. On the rolling hills the sheep went softly, and in vacant valleys cropped the lush verdure of the springtime, or in summer sought a scanty sustenance in the sun-dried grasses.

Intrepid men had pushed the railroad through the forbidding barrier of the Sierras, giving for the first time easy access to California, and thus making inevitable a changed manner of life and conditions.

I am a child of California, a grandchild of Maine, and a great-grandchild of Massachusetts. Fashions in ancestry change. When I chose mine straight American was still very correct; so I might as well admit at once that I am of American colonial stock, Massachusetts variety.

Up in the branches of my ancestral tree I find a normal number of farmers, sea-captains, small manufacturers, squires, justices of the peace and other town officers, members of the general court, privates in the militia, majors, colonels, one ghost, one governor, and seven passengers on that early emigrant ship, the *Mayflower;* but a great shortage of ministers, there being only one.

How I happened to be born so far away from the home of my ancestors, the type of life lived here on the frontier by a transplanted New England family, and the conditions that prevailed in California in the period between the mining rush and the tourist rush, is the story I shall tell.

The usual things had happened down the years on the east coast, —births, marryings, many children, death; new generations, scatterings, the settling and the populating of new land. Mother's people stayed close to their original Plymouth corner, but father's had frequently moved on to new frontiers. They went into Maine about the time of the Revolution, when it was still a wilderness, and then, by the middle of the next century, they were all through the opening west. It was a saying in the family that it was possible to drive from home into the far middle west, stopping over every night at the house of some cousin.

My father was Llewellyn Bixby of Norridgewock, Maine, and my mother was Mary Hathaway, youngest daughter of Reverend George Whitefield Hathaway, my one exception to the non-ministerial rule of the family. And he was this by force of his very determined mother, Deborah Winslow, who had made up her mind that her handsome young son should enter the profession at that time the most respected in the community. She was a woman called "set as the everlasting hills," and so determined was she that Whitefield should not be lured off into ways of business that she would not allow him to be taught arithmetic. Like the usual boy he rebelled at dictation, and when at Brown University became a leader in free-thinking circles, but suddenly was converted and accepted his mother's dictum. His own choice would have been to follow in the footsteps of his father, Washington Hathaway, a graduate of Brown University, 1798, and a lawyer. His sermons showed his inheritance of a legal mind, and he exhibited always a tolerance and breadth of spirit that were doubtless due to the tempering of his mother's orthodoxy by his gentle father's unitarianism. She, dear lady, would not have her likeness made by the new daguerreotype process lest she break the command, "Thou shalt not make unto thee any graven image, nor any likeness of anything—."

Grandfather was graduated from Williams College in 1827. I have his diploma with its faded blue ribbon and college seal; and, perhaps more personal and interesting, his "Commencement piece, a conference: Reputation as depending on genius, application and circumstance." This was discussed in turn by G. W. Hathaway, W. Lewis and B. B. Beckwith, it falling to the lot of grandfather to advocate the fundamental need of genius in the building of success.

After college he attended Andover Seminary, was ordained to the ministry and accepted a call to the parish church of Bloomfield (Skowhegan), Maine, a position which he held for a generation. While at Andover the portrait now cherished by his family was painted by one of his friends.

In Bloomfield there lived two orphan daughters of William Locke and Susannah Patterson, Mary and Anne, both of them young school teachers, and both destined to become the wife of the handsome young minister—Mary, the mother of his children, two sons and six daughters, Anne, their second mother. These Locke girls were the friends of the young Doles who went to the far Sandwich Islands. The first Dole boy born there was named George Hathaway in remembrance of my grandfather, and the first Hathaway girl child was Emily Ballard in honor of Mrs. Dole.

It was in the Locke house that the young couple set up their *lares* and *penates* and it was there I visited when I was a baby. It was from there that grandfather and his daughter Martha set out after forty-four years to join the rest of the family that had settled in California. And in my treasure chest beside the boy's college oration and diploma lies a copy of a farewell sermon written just fifty years later.

My aunt, Martha Hathaway, tells of her father as a "knightly soul," ever helpful, ever brave to espouse causes in which he believed, were they popular or not.

When little modest Lucy Stone came to Skowhegan to speak on "Woman's Rights" she met an unbelieving and heartily disapproving audience. Young Mr. Hathaway was the only minister in town to go on the platform with her. He presented her to the audience.

Another unpopular "cause" he espoused was that of temperance, and my aunt recalls from her childhood his return from a speaking trip in a terrible blizzard when his buffalo coat was fringed with icicles and he was dangerously chilled. I spent a Christmas week in that town myself once when the thermometer registered forty-five degrees below zero.

The home was also a station on the "underground railway" and stories have come down of exciting episodes and narrow escapes of dark travelers. There are tales also of interrupted attempts to hold anti-slavery meetings in the church in competition with horns and bangings of pew doors and beatings on the outer walls of the wooden building. When the war came Mr. Hathaway served for two years as chaplain of the Nineteenth Regiment of Maine Volunteers. I have a German testament that he used at this time. Before he left Maine he was for several terms a member of the state legislature. And in this later period he spent one year in Grinnell, Iowa, and one in his old home in Assonet, Massachusetts. He lived fourteen years in Southern California, the last nine in our home.

My father's family had been in Maine for a longer time, his two great-grandfathers, Samuel Bixby and Joseph Weston, going in from Massachusetts about 1770, and settling on the Kennebec River. Joseph Weston took his eleven-year-old son with him in the spring to find a location and prepare for his family to come in the fall. In September he left his boy and another of fourteen in charge of the cattle and cabin and went home to get his wife and other children. But he was balked in his purpose because of the setting in of an early winter and consequent freezing of the river highway. The boys had to stay alone in the woods caring for the cattle until spring made travel possible. When the family arrived they found the boys and cattle in good shape, the boys evidently being excellent Yankee pioneers.

By the middle of the nineteenth century Somerset County was full of Bixbys and Westons. When Rufus Bixby entertained at Thanksgiving dinner on one occasion he had one hundred fifty-six guests, all kin-folk. He was a brother of my grandfather, Amasa Bixby, the two of them having married sisters, Betsey and Fanny Weston. A third sister, Electa Weston, married William Reed Flint and became the mother of the two cousins who were father's business associates all during his California life.

The Maine farms were becoming crowded and there was no land in the neighborhood left for the young folks. Father was one of an even hundred grandchildren of Benjamin Weston and Anna Powers, a sample of the prevalent size of families at that time. The early American farmers were not essentially of the soil, but were driven by the necessities of a new country to wring support from the land. At the first opportunity to escape into callings where more return for less physical output promised, they fled the farms. I remember that my uncle Jotham who had rather short stumpy fingers used to maintain that he had worn them down in his boyhood gathering up stones in the home pastures and piling them into walls.

In the spring of 1851, Llewellyn Bixby, an erect, square-shouldered young man of twenty-five, with gray eyes and black hair, was studying engineering at Waterville. He had finished his education at a district school and Bloomfield Academy some time before and had taught, had farmed, had even undertaken the business of selling books from house to house, for which latter effort he confessed he did not seem to have the requisite qualities. He then determined to go into engineering, a field of growing opportunity. One day his father appeared unexpectedly at the door of a shop where he was at work, with the proposal that he join his brother Amasa and his cousin, Dr. Thomas Flint, in a trip to California, whither the latter's brother, Benjamin, had gone in 1849.

The plan appealed to him and he returned to Norridgewock with his father, to make an immediate start for that far-off coast which was to prove his home for the rest of his life.

It was July, 1851, just too late to be technically called pioneers, that they reached San Francisco, but to all intents and purposes they belong to that group of early comers to this state who have had so large a part in determining its destiny.

The next year, two more of my father's brothers, Marcellus and Jotham, ventured around the Horn, and ultimately the rest of the children followed,—Amos, Henry, Solomon, George, Francina and Nancy, (Mrs. William Lovett), making in all eight brothers and two sisters. Amos, who was the last to come, was a lawyer and editor and had been instrumental in the founding of Grinnell College in Iowa and the University of Colorado in Boulder as he made his gradual progress from Maine to California. He founded and edited the first newspaper in Long Beach.

William and Augustus Rufus, sons of Rufus Bixby were here for a number of years during the fifties. Thomas Flint Bixby, Augustus Simon, John W. and Eulalia, children of Simon Bixby, came very early and made California their permanent home. I know there were others of whom I have no record.

Allen Bixby, once state commander of the American Legion, is the grandson of Amasa, the brother who accompanied my father in the first trip across the isthmus. It is this sort of bodily transplanting of young stock that has left so many of the New England counties bereft of former names, but has built up in new communities many of the customs and traditions of the older civilization.

Not only did my father's immediate family come to this state but also many of his friends and cousins. I am told that at the presidential election in 1860 all the men in Paso Robles who voted for Lincoln came from Somerset County, Maine.

Because this migration is typical and because many of these cousins made names for themselves beyond the limits of the family, I am going to mention a few of them.

Among them was, for instance, Dr. Mary Edmands, who was an early physician in San Francisco in the days when it took grit as well as brains for a woman to gain a medical education. She succeeded as a mother as well as a professional woman, her sons and daughter at present standing high in their respective callings.

Nathan Blanchard of Santa Paula was a son of a fourth Weston sister, Eunice. He, after many hardships and almost unbelievable patience, made a success of lemon culture in Southern California, and worked out the fundamental principle of curing the fruit that is now in vogue wherever lemons are grown for market.

Another name widely known is that of Mrs. Frank Gibson, the daughter of another cousin. She has been a leader among women for many years, and member of the State Board of Immigration. Her son, Hugh Gibson, is at present United States Ambassador to Belgium.

These are but a few of the several hundred from this one Maine family who are scattered up and down this western land.

CHAPTER II

The Very Little Girl

I W A S born, as I have said, on a sheep ranch in the central part of California during its pastoral period, but it is doubtless true that the environment and influences about me during the first few months of my life were very little different from what they would have been had my Maine mother not left her New England home about a year before my birth.

But as the months passed and the circle of my experience widened, I was more and more affected by the conditions of my own time and place.

My first memory relates to an experience characteristic of a frontier country in which the manner of life is still primitive. I remember very distinctly sitting in my mother's lap in a stage-coach and being unbearably hot and thirsty. After I was a grown girl my father took me with him to inspect the last remaining link of the old stage lines (between Santa Barbara and Santa Ynez), that formerly ran up and down the state from San Diego to San Francisco, and I, being reminded of that long ride in my babyhood, asked him about it. He told me that on the return trip to San Juan after my first visit to Los Angeles, instead of going north by steamer they had traveled by stage through the San Joaquin Valley, encountering the worst heat he had ever experienced in California. Then he added that I could not possibly remember anything about it since I was only eleven months old when it happened. I maintain, however, that I do, because the picture and the sense of heat are too vivid to be a matter of hearsay alone. I was so small that my head came below my mother's shoulder as I leaned against her outside arm at the left end of the middle seat. There were no other women in the stage, papa was behind us, and opposite were three men, who were sorry for me and talked to me.

The months went by and I came to know my home. It was among rolling hills whose velvety slopes bounded my world. Over all was the wide blue sky, a bit of it having fallen into a nearby hollow.

This was a fascinating pond, for water ran uphill beside the road to get into it. Then there were many fish, none of which ever would get caught on my bent-pin hook. It was into this water that I once saw some little ducks jump, and, like many of the younger generation, greatly alarm their mother, who, being a hen, had no understanding of her children's adjustment to strange conditions.

The San Justo house was newly built by the three partner-cousins, large enough to accommodate their families. It was reminiscent of Maine, with its white paint, green blinds and sharp gables edged with wooden lace, something like the perforated paper in the boxes of perfumed toilet soap,—perhaps meant to remind them of icicles. The house and all the auxiliary buildings were built on rising ground, so that under each one, on the lower side, was a high basement, usually enclosed by a lattice. Under the veranda that extended across the front of the house was a fine place to play, with many treasures to be found, among them sacks of the strange beet seed, reminders of an early interest in sugar-making, and sweet potatoes that are very good for nibbling raw; they taste like chestnuts.

At the rear of this house was a low porch, without a railing, where the carriages drove up many times a day, for, with the large family, the wide acres, and active business, there was much coming and going. This veranda served as an annex to the dining room. In those days fruit came after breakfast instead of before, and it was here that we ate it, tossing the squeezed oranges and the scalloped watermelon rinds into a conveniently placed box that was frequently emptied.

Directly back of the kitchen was a small building containing a storeroom where Dick and I were accustomed to climb the shelves like a ladder for packages of sweet chocolate, while Aunt Francina, oblivious, skimmed the many large milk pans. In the building also was a laundry, containing a stove upon which I have seen soft-soap made and tallow prepared for the candle moulds. In a corner, made by this house and a retaining wall, was a large sand pile, and from the great oak on the bank above hung a long swing. I wonder if it is any more delightful for an old person to penetrate the sky in an aeroplane than for a little girl to do the same when pushed by the strong arm of her father!

Down towards the pond was the horse barn, with its long rows of stalls on one side, and its shelter for the carts and buggies beside the hay-mow on the other. I was warned of dangerous heels and

MARY HATHAWAY BIXBY, MY MOTHER

RANCHO SAN JUSTO, ABOUT 1865

was duly circumspect, but liked to get, occasionally, a nice fresh long hair from a tail for purposes of scientific experiment. I was going to turn a hair into a snake if possible. In a similar attempt to verify popular statements I spent many an hour with salt in my hand, trailing birds.

On one of my ventures behind the horses I was rewarded by the discovery of a very heavy little bottle, standing on a dark ledge. It contained mercury. Great was my joy to get a few drops in my hand, to divide them into the tiniest globules, and then to watch them coalesce into one little silvery pool.

The building standing back up the hill was the one in which the imported Spanish merino sheep were kept. I seldom went there, but in the corral behind the barn next lower several cows stood every night to be milked, among them Old Muley, my friend, on whose broad back I often sat astride while the process was going on. There were large, pink-blossomed mallows bordering the fences and this barn, and under the latter many white geese could be seen between the slats of the open siding. How excited I was when the day for gathering the feathers came!

The hired men occupied the original ranch house; in the usual basement was the tool room, open to us children. I here learned to hammer, saw and plane, and, most charming of all, bore air holes with an auger in the wooden boxes we used in the making of figure-four traps. I also learned about gimlets, chisels, pliers, brads, rivets, and screws and thus prepared myself to be a general handy man at college and in my own home. It was in this shop that papa made me a fire-cracker holder,—a willow stick with a hole bored in one end in which to place the lovely red symbol of patriotism, so that I could celebrate without endangering my fingers.

In front of the house was the flower garden, enclosed by a white picket fence as a protection against chickens and other wandering ranch animals. Ladies-delights turned up their smiling faces beside one walk, and nearby grew papa's favorites, cinnamon pinks. I liked the red honey-suckle and the dark mourning-brides that were like velvet cushions stuck full of white-headed pins. There was one orange tree that bore no fruit important enough for me to remember, but, in spring, had many waxy white blossoms that smelled so good it made one hurt inside.

In larger enclosures, bounded by the same white fencing, grew vegetables and fruit trees. Sometimes we pulled a pungent horse-radish root and pretended that a bite of it made us crazy, an excuse for much running and wild gesticulation. Under a long row of loaded blackberry vines Dick once asked me the riddle, "Why is a blackberry like a newspaper?" Do you know the answer? It is: "Both are black and white and red all over." I presume the play upon the word "red" was my introduction to puns.

The orchard contained peaches, plums, pears, apples, and apricots, but to my mind the cherry trees were the chief glory. One evening while Annie Mooney, our nurse, was taking in some clothes from the line, my little sister and I had a feast of fallen cherries, but she ate with less discrimination than I, for when, a few minutes later, we drank our supper milk she had convulsions. A quick immersion in a tub of hot water cured her, and we had learned about babies and cherries and milk all mixed up together.

Down in the far corner of the orchard was a spring, with marshy ground about it, where the children were forbidden to go. But one morning, bored by the lack of novelty in our lives, one of the Flint twins and I boldly ventured into the tabooed region. We had hardly arrived when we saw an enormous black snake, which drove us back in terror, chasing us, with glittering eyes and darting tongue, over the ridges and hollows of the new-ploughed ground that clutched at our feet as if in collusion with the black dragon guard of the spring. I laid, during those few minutes, the foundation for many a horror-stricken dream. The snake was real. I wonder if the pursuit was merely the imagining of a guilty conscience.

Beyond the summer house, beyond the fence and at the hilltop end of a little grassy path, was the family burying ground, where, under the wild flowers, lay a few baby cousins who had gone away before I came, and papa's young brother, Solomon, who, while reading poetry in a lonely sheep camp, had been shot to death by some unknown hand.

Our home was in a little valley with no other houses in sight, but a mile and a half away, down a hill and across a bridge, lay the old town of San Juan Bautista, with its post-office, store, adobe inn and its homes, a medley of Spanish and American types. The mission church with its long corridor, arched and tile-paved, and its garden, where peacocks used to walk and drop their shining feathers for a little girl to pick up, was the dominating feature of the place, its very cause for being. Inside was dim silence; there were strange dark pictures on the walls, and burning candles, a very large music book with big square notes, and a great Bible, chained to its desk.

There was another church in San Juan, one that was wooden,

light, bare and small, where I learned from a tiny flowered card, "Blessed are the peacemakers," which, being interpreted for my benefit, meant, "Sallie mus'n't quarrel with little sister." I ate up a rosebud and wriggled in my seat during the long sermon and wondered about the lady who brushed her hair smooth and low on one side and high on the other. Had she only one ear?

I have been told that my church attendance involved certain distractions for my fellow-worshippers, and that my presence was tolerated only because of the desirability of training me in correct Sunday habits. On one occasion my restlessness led me into disaster. My parents had gone to the chancel, carrying my little sister Anne for her christening, leaving me in the pew. It was a strange performance. The minister took the baby in his arms, and then put something from a silver bowl on her forehead, and began to pray. I must know what was in the bowl! Everybody had shut-eyes, so there was a good chance for me to find out without troubling anyone. I darted forward and managed to discover that the mysterious something was water, for I spilled it over myself.

The trip to church was made in a two-seated, low carriage, with a span of horses, while my everyday rides with papa were in a single buggy, but with two horses also, for we had far to go and liked going fast. Sometimes we went to Gilroy, and sometimes to Hollister, often just about the ranch to the various sheep camps, which were widely separated.

I began these business trips almost as soon as I was old enough to sit up alone. When we started I would be very erect and alert at papa's side, but before long I would droop and be retired to the bottom of the buggy, where, wrapped in a robe, and with his foot for a pillow, I would sleep contentedly for hours. I remember my disgust when I had grown so long that I must change my habit and put my legs back under the seat, instead of lying across in the correct way. I objected to change, but was persuaded that it would be inconvenient for me to get tangled, during some pleasant dream, in the actualities of the spokes of a moving wheel.

At one time papa and I were very much occupied clearing a field, a piece of work which he must have reserved for himself, since there were no other men about. He also enjoyed chopping wood and this may have been his "daily dozen." We cut down several large oak trees, cleared out underbrush, and, piling it up against the great stumps, built fires that roared for a time and then smouldered for days.

Sometimes I walked with mamma on the hills back of the house, and when we were tired we would sit down under a tree and she would tell me a story and make me a chaplet of oak leaves, folding and fastening each leaf to the next in a most ingenious way. If our walk took us into the lower lands she made bewitching little baskets from the rushes that grew near the water's edge. I also found the strange equisetum, that I sometimes called "horse-tail," and sometimes "stove-pipe," which latter I preferred, because none of the horses that I knew had disjointable tails, while the little hollow tubes of stem that fitted into each other so well must serve the fairies most excellently for their chimneys.

Several spring mornings as I grew older, I got up at dawn with mamma, went to the early empty kitchen for a drink of milk, and then went out with her for a horseback ride, she in her long broadcloth habit and stiff silk hat, and I, a tiny timid girl, perched on a side-saddle atop a great horse. From the point of view of horsemanship I was not a great success, but the joy of the dawn air, the rising sun, the wild-flowers, the companionship of my mother is mine forever.

It was on one of these morning expeditions when we were comparing notes about our tastes in colors, that I found she liked a strange shade of red that to me looked unattractive. I was overwhelmed by the thought that perhaps it did not look the same to both of us, and that if I saw it as she did I might like it also; but there was no way for either of us to know how it actually looked to the other! I realized the essential isolation of every human being. However, I forgot the loneliness when papa joined us on the road beside the pond, where the wild lilac scattered its blue-violet lace on the over-hanging bank. He cut for me a willow whistle that sounded the shrill joy of being alive.

On the Sunday afternoon walks when we all went up into the hills together I learned, among other classics:

"Little drops of water,
  Little grains of sand,
Make a mighty ocean
  And the wondrous land."

But it was at night when I was safely put in my bed that I heard through the open door, mamma, at the parlor piano, singing to me:

"I want to be an angel,
  And with the angels stand,

A crown upon my head,
A harp within my hand."

I suppose that neither she nor I were really in immediate haste for the fulfillment of that wish, but it made a good bed-time song. Another favorite was, *Shall we Gather at the River?*, and there was occasionally a somber one called *Pass Under the Rod*.

My bed was a very safe place, for did not angels guard it, "two at the foot, and two at the head"? I knew who my angels were,—my very own grandmother, who had died when my mother was a new baby, the aunt for whom I had been named, my little cousin Mary who really should have been guarding her brother Harry, and a fourth whom I have now forgotten.

The songs were not gay, but my life was not troubled by thoughts of death. Heaven seemed a nice place, somewhere, and angels and fairies were normal parts of my universe.

I did have a few minor troubles. My language was criticized. "You bet your boots" did not meet with maternal approval. Then, if I carelessly put my sunbonnet strings into my mouth, I got my tongue burned from the vinegar and cayenne pepper into which they had been dipped for the express purpose of making the process disagreeable. Those sunbonnets, with which my head was sheathed every time I started out into the airy out-of-doors, were my chief pests. I usually compromised my integrity by untying the strings as soon as I was out of sight. I would double back the corners of the bonnet, making it into a sort of cocked hat with a bow on top, made from the hated strings, thus letting my poor scratched ears out of captivity.

My cousin, Mrs. Gibson, tells me that she also suffered the martyrdom of sunbonnets; I presume in those days girls were supposed to preserve natural complexions, it not being considered decent to have recourse to vanity boxes. Her mother was more ingenious than mine in making sure that her child did not jeopardize her skin. She made buttonholes in the top of the bonnet through which she drew strands of hair and braided them outside the bonnet, thus insuring it against removal.

Papa and I went to the circus on every possible occasion. Once, at Hollister, I saw General and Mrs. Tom Thumb, Minnie Warren and Commodore Nutt, whose photograph — with Mr. Barnum — I have preserved. Minnie Warren was said to be the size of a six-year-old, but the standard for six-year-olds must have come out of the east. I was several inches taller than she.

A pretty lady, dressed in pink tarleton skirts, who rode several horses at a time, and jumped through tissue paper hoops, was my first heroine. Dick and I kept her picture for months on a ledge under the office desk, and there rendered her frequent homage.

The mention of this desk calls to mind other activities centering in that office. On one occasion, when I was suitably young, the spirit moved me to carry a shovelful of live coals out through the door to the porch, and there coax up a fire by the addition of kindling wood. The same spirit, or another, however, suggested a compensating action. I summoned my mother to see my "nice fire," to the salvation of the house.

Fire, candles, matches, revolvers, all held a fascination. It is evident that neither my cousin Harry nor I were intended for a violent death, for it was our custom to investigate from time to time his father's loaded revolver, turning the chambers about and removing and replacing the cartridges. Our faith in our ability to handle the dangerous weapon safely seems to have been justified by our success.

It was deemed wise to keep me occupied, so far as possible, in order to thwart Satan, ever on the lookout for idle hands. So I was taught to sew patchwork and to knit, to read and to spell. There were short periods when I had to stay in the house, but like all California children, I spent out-of-doors most of the time not given over to eating and sleeping. Now-a-days even those duties are attended to upon porches.

Under mamma's guidance I once laboriously and secretly sewed "over and over" a gray and white striped "comfort bag" for a birthday gift to papa. It was modelled on the bags made for the soldiers in the Union army when my mother was a girl. We made a special trip to Hollister to buy its contents, black and white thread, coarse needles, buttons, wax, blunt scissors, and to top off, pink and white sugary peppermint drops. That bag remained in service for twenty years, going always in father's satchel whenever he went away. It came to my rescue once when I had torn my skirt from hem to band. As he sewed up the rent for me with nice big stitches, first on one side and then on the other, he told me it was a shoemaker's stitch and had the advantage of bringing the edges together just as they had been originally, without puckering the cloth. Mamma used the same stitch to mend the torn pages of books and sheet music, in those days before Mr. Dennison invented his transparent tape.

Time went by slowly, slowly, as it does when one is young. All day there was play, except for the occasional stint of patchwork, or the reading lesson, — every day but Sunday, with its church in the forenoon and stories and walks in the afternoon. Mamma would say, "When I was a little girl in Maine," until to me Maine meant Paradise. In that country there was a brook where one could wade, and the great river, on whose banks in the woods children could picnic and hunt for wild berries, — what a charm in the words, "going berrying"! Even the nest of angry hornets with their sharp stings did not lessen my enthusiasm. At San Justo there were no Martha and Susan, no Julia and Ella for me to play with, — just boys, (who seemed to answer very well for little tom-boy Sallie when Maine was not in mind).

When I heard of snow and sleighs and sleds and the wonderful attic with its cunning low curtained windows and the doll colony who lived there, I forgot the charms of the ranch and the boy play. It was nothing to me that there were horses and cows, ducks, geese and chickens. It was nothing to me that Dick and I could make figure-four traps, and, walking beyond the wool-barn, set them on the hillside for quail; that once we had the excitement of finding our trap upset, our captives gone, and great bear tracks all about. The long sunny days of freedom with the boys, the great herds of sheep that came up for shearing, the many rides with my father through the lovely valleys and over the hills were commonplace, just what I had always known. No, life in California was very tame compared with the imagined joys of Maine.

CHAPTER III

Down in Maine

TWICE mamma took me to Maine to see grandmother and grandfather and Aunt Martha, once when I was two-and-a-half years old and once when I was nearly five. In each case we stayed about six months so that I became acquainted with New England in all its varying seasons.

Perhaps it was the being there just when I was forming habits of speech that has fastened upon me an unmistakable New England way of speaking, however much the pure dialect may have been corrupted by my usual western environment.

My aunt tells me that when she first saw me she could think of nothing so much as a little frisking squirrel, my dark eyes were so shining and I darted about so constantly. I couldn't wait after my arrival at the strange place even long enough to take off hood and coat before demanding scissors with which to cut paper dolls. When the outer wraps were removed, the interested relatives saw a slender little girl, with straight yellow hair, brown eyes and a smooth skin, tanned by wind and sun.

Evidently there was much excitement attendant upon reaching grandmother's, for when I was tucked away for a nap, with a brand new book purchased the day before in Boston to entertain me until sleep should come, I occupied myself with tearing every page into pieces the size of a quarter. I have no suggestion to offer as to why I did it. When the situation came to adult attention, papa sat down on the trunk beside the crib and gave me the only spanking he was ever known to bestow upon his family. The rope was behind the trunk. I saw it while lying across his knees.

The ill-fated book was not the only purchase made in Boston. Mamma and I had our pictures taken, and bought clothes for the cold winter ahead. I had a bottle-green dress and a bottle-green coat to match, also stockings and bonnet. They put me up on the counter to try the things on me, and I was glad when mamma chose the velvet bonnet with a white ruche and little pink roses, for I liked it best of all. Then there were kid gloves, dark green and white, both of which I hated, because my poor little fingers buckled when they were put on. When I was taken to call on the cousins in Beacon Street, I was dressed up in all the regalia, even to the white gloves. Alas, there was a coping beside the steps, just the right height for a hand-rail for me, and unfortunately, dust is black even in Boston. Missy was in disgrace when she reached the front door. She was better adapted to play in mud pies than to make formal calls.

Even if I liked dirt and freedom, I also liked clothes well enough to remember those I have had, so that now I would venture to reconstruct a continuous series of them, extending back to babyhood. An early favorite was of scarlet cashmere, cut in "Gabrielle" style, with scalloped neck, sleeves and hem, buttonholed with black silk, and on the front an embroidered bunch of barley, acorns and roses. With this dress went a little white fur overcoat, cap and muff, all trimmed with a narrow edge of black fur. So much for clothes. They were ordinarily buried under aprons.

Maine was a wonderful place! The leaves on the trees were red and yellow, brown and purple, instead of green, and when the wind blew they fell off. It left the trees very queer, but the dry leaves on the ground made a fine swishing noise when one scuffed in them, and when a little breeze picked them up and sent them scurrying after one they looked like the rats following the Pied Piper of Hamelin. Mamma gathered some of the prettiest, pressed them and waxed them with a hot iron and a paraffine candle. We took them back to San Justo with us and pinned them on the lace curtains, to remind us of Skowhegan.

Whenever we went to town on an errand or to church, we crossed the bridge, under which the great river rushed to pour over the falls below, a never failing wonder. On the far side of the island the water turned the wheels for Cousin Levi Weston's sawmill, an interesting, if dangerous, place to visit.

We had not been long in Maine before the air filled with goose feathers, only it wasn't feathers, but wet snow. Then came sleds and sleighs, a snow man and Christmas, with a piggy-back ride on grandfather to see the tree at the church.

The snow was so deep on the ground and it was so cold, the chickens had to stay in the barn all the time; every morning grandmother and I took my little red bucket and went to feed them, out through the summer kitchen, the wood-shed, past the horse's stall to their house.

While I was in Maine I learned odors as well as sights. I know the smell of snow in the air, of pine trees in winter, of a woodshed and barn, of an old house that has been lived in for long, long years. I came to know the fragrance of a cellar, apples and butter, vegetables and preserves, and can recall its clammy coolness.

To have a bath in a wash-tub by the kitchen stove was a lark for a little wild-westerner who had known only a modern bathroom. The second time we were at grandfather's there was a curious soft-rubber pouch for a tub, which was set up when wanted before the fire in the north bedroom. The bottom rested on the floor, while the sides were held up by poles, resting on chairs. After a week-end tubbing, mamma and I would say together,

> "How pleasant is Saturday night
>   When all the week I've been good,
> Said never a word that was cross
>   And done all the good that I could."

I have other memories of that fire-place. Once, during the first visit, mamma left me for a few days in the care of my inexperienced aunt, of whom I took advantage. I assured her that my mother every night rubbed my chest with camphorated oil and gave me a spoonful of Hive's cough syrup. Evidently I had recently enjoyed a cold. So every night I got my oil rub and the sweet sticky dose, and, wrapped in an old shawl and called a "little brown sausage," was rocked during some blissful minutes of story-telling. Mamma was shocked when she returned to find the empty bottle and to know the whereabouts of its contents.

Still another fireplace memory, — papa was taking care of me in this room, and was having so good a time reading and smoking with his chair tipped back and his feet high against the mantel that I thought I would do the same. I climbed up and took from the mantel a pretty twisted paper lamp-lighter, then seated myself beside him, put my feet as high as I could on my side of the fire-place, adjusted my newspaper, lighted my squill cigar, and in mouthing it about, managed to set my front hair on fire. That attracted papa's attention to his job.

Soon the time approached for us to be starting west again. Hardly had we reached Chicago when there was a dangerous fire in the business section; it was not so long after the great fire that people had forgotten the terror and panic of it. So we must flee the hotel, although papa kept saying that if men would tear up the carpets and wet them and hang them outside the building they might save it. Mamma dressed me and packed the trunk as fast as she could, and I went out into the hall and looked down the elevator well, where the door had been left open. It was the first chance I had ever had to see what a deep hole it was, but mamma called me to come back, and I thought she was frightened to see me leaning over and looking down. We went away in Uncle Jo's buggy through streets filled with pushing shouting people, and, as we looked back, all the sky was red with fire. We went to a small boarding house over by the lake, and all there was in it was a red balloon, many mosquitoes and a wonderful talking doll that the dear uncle brought me.

San Francisco came next, a few days at the Grand Hotel, a ride on the octagonal street car that diagonaled off from Market Street, to visit Woodward's Gardens, and then home by train and stage. It was good after all to get back to California. Here was our own sitting room, with its white marble mantel, its dainty flowered carpet and its lace curtains. On the wall were colored pictures of Yosemite and a Sunset at Sea, and engravings of *L'Allegro* and *Il Penseroso*, all hanging by crimson cords with tassels. I liked the dancing girl better, but mamma preferred the sad one.

I was also glad to get back to my old toys, my book about *Ten Little Indians*, and the boy cousins who lived at the other end of the house. And here, soon, came little sister, who was the cunningest baby that ever was. They rolled her up so close in blankets that Aunt Francina was afraid she would be smothered. I didn't want her to be smothered. What a long time it does take for a baby to grow up enough to play with a person born three years ahead of her!

Two years later mamma took me and little Anne back again to Maine, for she had had letters telling her that grandmother was very ill. It was a harder trip with two children and so my mother planned to simplify it in every possible way. She invented for us traveling dresses of a medium brown serge, with bloomers to match, a whole generation before such dresses came into general favor for little girls. With these, fewer bags and satchels were necessary, and we looked as well dressed at the end as at the beginning of the journey; and, moreover, I was able to stand on my head modestly, whenever I felt like it. I am glad that I did not have to be mother of restless me on such a long, confined trip; I am also glad that restless I had a mother who could cut out such fascinating paper boxes and tell stories and think of thousands of things to do.

Perhaps having two children to take care of kept mamma from grieving so much about her mother.

I realized little about the illness, because, except for a daily good-morning call, we children were kept out of the sick room, usually playing out-of-doors. We rolled down the grassy slope in the south yard, or drove about in the low basket phaeton along the winding, shady roads. Sometimes we had a picnic, — I remember especially the one on my fifth birthday. Georgie Hill, who helped Aunt Martha with the housework, made a wonderful cake, which contained a button, a thimble, a penny, and a ring; in some very satisfying way, the section containing the ring came to me. I had always wanted a ring. I was happy, happy, and then the very next day I lost it, making mud pies with Annie Allen. I never had another ring until I was grown up, not even a bracelet, which might have consoled me. But if I had had either I probably would have had to suffer the sorrows of separation, since it was my habit to lose my treasures. My gold pins are sowed up and down the earth; my sister still has everyone she owned. Perhaps it was in recognition of my capacity to mislay things, and to encourage stoical acceptance of the situation, that led grandfather to write in my autograph album:

"My little granddaughter,
Just do as you ought to,
Neither worry nor fret
At what can't be mended,
Nor wait to regret
Till doing is ended."

It was on this same birthday that Elizabeth came to me, and her I have not lost. She was a doll almost as tall as I, that had been made by my great-grandmother, Deborah Hathaway, for her son's little girls. The doll came last to my mother, who was the youngest, and from her descended to me. Elizabeth had a cloth body, stuffed with cotton, white kid arms and hands and a papier-mache head. She was so unfortunate soon after her arrival in California, as to suffer a fracture of the skull, due to contact with a hammer wielded by my small sister. Elizabeth survived the grafting on of a china head, and is now eighty or more years old, but looking as young as ever.

I possess many letters written to my father by my mother at this time, from which I can gain ideas regarding what manner of woman she was, to supplement my own memory of her whom I lost while still a child.

I seem to have been something of a puzzle to my gentle mother. I quote from one letter:

"Sarah . . . the strangest child I ever saw . . . so affectionate, but will not be coaxed . . . super-abundance of spirits. . . She tries to remember all the new rules of life [I was five years old] . . . brown eyes. I hope those eyes will not hold a shadow caused by her mother misunderstanding her and crushing out in her by sternness anything sweet and beautiful. I would not want to love her so fondly as to make a foolish, conceited woman of her, but I don't know that that is any worse than to give her life a gloomy start."

I love this letter. It delights me that my mother, a high-bred New England lady, to whom foolishness and frivolity were anathema, should prefer even them to harshness and a broken spirit for her little daughter. However, her desire to give my life a happy start was not incompatible with good discipline. She expected obedience and got it, sometimes in very ingenious ways. On one occasion when I had been fretful — "whining" she called it, — she suggested that as I was usually a good girl and did what she wanted it must be that I was really unable to improve my voice, that my throat must be rusty and in need of oil to cure the squeak, so she proceeded to grease the inside of it with olive oil applied on the end of a stripped white feather. Do you wonder that it was years before I learned to like French salad dressing, with its reminder of disordered vocal cords?

In the later summer grandmother died, but as we had seen so little of her and were kept away from the evidences and symbols of death, it did not make much impression upon us.

We stayed on in Skowhegan until papa was free to come to Maine for us. In the meantime both mamma and Aunt Martha visited the Centennial and their reports of its sights and wonders made me most anxious to go to Philadelphia, also. When it was proposed that our return trip should be made by way of that city, in order that my father might visit the exposition I was delighted, but when he arrived and said he could not, on account of the state of his business affairs, I received one of the great disappointments of my life. I shall never forget my unavailing efforts to persuade them that they ought not to make me miss that Centennial, since I could not possibly live a hundred years for the next one.

Soon after we left the old home was sold, and grandfather and Aunt Martha moved to California, where the rest of us lived. The man who bought the place cut down the beautiful trees, tore down the house and built two small ones in its stead. But although the original house is gone in fact it will live in my mind so long as I do. I could draw its floor plan; I could set much of its furniture in the correct position.

The arrangement of the dining-room was for years very important for me, because the only way I could distinguish my right hand from my left was by seating myself in imagination beside grandfather at table where I was when I first learned which was which, — left toward him, right toward cellar door. And, being so seated, I recall another lesson, — vinegar should not be called "beginniger."

It was in the south yard that we built the big snow man; it was there that the sleigh upset when we turned in from the street with too much of a flourish, and pitched Nan and me deep into a snow bank; it was here under the apple trees that we turned somersaults; it was here that the horse stood on his hind legs to shake down his favorite apples from the tree. The same horse would come to the stone door-step by the kitchen and rattle the bucket there when he was thirsty; that was the doorstep where I placed my feet when papa made my little shoes shine like his boots; and here Elizabeth was placed in grandfather Weston's old clock-case for her long ride to California, — as if she were going in a coffin to heaven. But the San Justo heaven lacked the great beds of lilies-of-the-valley, such as grew under the trees in the Maine yard.

These impressions were planted deep in my mind during the months I spent in the beautiful village, with its dignified white houses, its tall trees, its great river. But, once again on my westward way, they slipped back into the files of memory, displaced by the renewal of other old impressions, for I was making my fourth trans-continental trip, my fourth stop in Chicago with my mother's brother, Josiah Hathaway.

What fun there was, riding a whole long week in a Pullman car with its many friendly people, and a new routine of life. In those days dining-cars, with leisurely meals and dainty service had not been discovered. There were irregular stops with only twenty minutes for refreshment, so that a child must depend largely on the luncheon basket. The bringing of the table and opening the tempting boxes and packages was a welcome break in the long day.

There were tall green bottles of queen olives, and pans packed with fried chicken, and all the bread and jam one might eat. We had a can of patent lemonade, — strange greenish sugar, needing only a few drops from the little bottle embedded in the powder, and train water to make it into ambrosia. Such a meal involved soiled hands, but even the washing of them had a new charm, for mamma took with her to the dressing-room a bottle of Murray and Lanman's Florida Water, a few drops of which in the alkali water made a milky bath fit for the hands of a princess.

When interest within the car failed there was the window, with its ever new pictures. If there were no houses or people, mountains or clouds to be seen, there might be a village of prairie dogs, and the rhythm of passing poles carrying the telegraph wires never failed. I saw cowboys on their dancing horses, and silent Indians, the women carrying on their backs little Hiawathas, and offering for sale bows and arrows or beaded moccasins.

Then night came, and with it the making of magic beds by the smiling black genie. Once, after I had been deposited behind the green curtains, we stopped at a way station, where, pressing my nose against the window pane, I saw by the light of a torch, a great buffalo head mounted on a pole, and many men moving in and out of the fitful light.

With groans and creakings, with bells and weird whistles we were soon on our way again, and, to the steady song of the wheel, in the swaying springy bed, I was being whisked over the plains in as many days as father had once spent in months driving the first sheep to California.

We went back to San Justo and stayed there forever; and then, when I was almost seven, we went south to the Cerritos for a never-to-be-forgotten summer with my cousin Harry. When fall came, instead of returning to the ranch at San Juan we moved to Los Angeles, a little city, and there I lived until both it and I grew up.

CHAPTER IV

Father's Story

S OON after we settled in Los Angeles I was very sick, due, I fear, to the hasty swallowing of half-chewed raisins when my foraging expedition to the pantry was menaced by an approaching mother. She did not know for several hours about my disobedience of her law against "swiping" food between meals, — if I were really hungry I would be glad to eat dry bread without butter or jam, — but the punishment for sin was as sure as it was in the Sunday school books. I sat for a long, long time screwed up in a little aching knot in front of the Franklin stove before I was ready to admit an excruciating pain. I think now-a-days it would have been called appendicitis.

The doctor took heroic measures: castor oil, tiny black stinking pills, steaming flannels wrung out of boiling vinegar and applied to my shrinking abdomen; awful, thick, nasty, white, sweetish cod-liver-oil. I survived.

I was only seven, and not used to staying in bed for a month at a time, so papa, sorry for me, day by day, told me the story of his life. He told me about his home, the brick farmhouse at Norridgewock on the Kennebec, the same river that I had seen when I was in Maine.

When he was a little boy there were no matches and no kitchen stoves, so that his mother had to cook before an open fireplace, and the clothes for all the family were made at home. His mother spun wool from their sheep and wove it into cloth and dyed it in the great indigo pot that stood when she was not using it just inside the shed door. When they killed a cow for beef they saved the hide, and then in the fall a traveling shoemaker came to the house and made boots for them, right there where they could watch him.

When papa was six he secretly learned to milk one of the cows and then with great joy exhibited his prowess, only to be informed that thereafter it was to be his daily chore. Another duty that fell to him about this time was to take care at night of each two-year-old whenever its place in the cradle was taken by a new baby. Somehow the oldest child in the family, Francina, managed to escape the usual fate of an oldest daughter, that of secondary mother.

The most wonderful hat that papa ever had was made by cutting down a white beaver of his father's — possibly a "Tippecanoe and Tyler too" campaign hat. Once when it was worn on a berrying expedition he hung it on the limb of a tree for safe-keeping — and then could never find the tree and precious hat again, a tragedy of youth.

Papa drew an amusing picture of himself at ten years of age in his "Sunday-go-to-meeting" clothes. His trousers came half-way between knee and ankle, his jacket was short and round, his collar so high he could not turn his head, although he could rest his neck during the long service by using his ears as hooks over the top of the collar. A stove-pipe hat completed the outfit.

During those evening stories while I was convalescing I learned many things about the boy's life in the far-away Maine, of his many cousins, of his schooling, and why he elected astronomy in place of French at Bloomfield Academy; of the years when he taught school or worked on a farm and then of his decision to go to California. He told me of the sea voyage and the stay in Panama, of San Francisco, and of the life in Volcano, the little mining town; of the return to Maine and of the journey west across the plains, driving sheep and cattle. He told me the story in detail until he reached Salt Lake City, and then one evening something intervened, I was well again and the absorbing tale was postponed and then again and again, never to be taken up.

Three years later, Uncle Ben, one of the travelers across the plains, died; in a few years more father was gone, and I suddenly realized how little I really knew of the venturesome expedition of the young men. So I wrote to Dr. Flint, the survivor, asking that he tell me something of their pioneer experience. He replied that he had kept diaries on both journeys and that I was welcome to see them at any time. But before the opportunity came he too had died, I was in the thick of a very busy life, and his letter was forgotten. Twenty years later I found it and immediately asked his son to see the journals, but their existence was not known. A holiday devoted to a search among old papers was rewarded by the discovery of the valuable documents.

And so, while I cannot recall all the detail of the charming tale my father told me, I am able, because of these records, to give an accurate report of how the cousins came to California and brought across plains, mountains, and deserts to this Pacific Coast some of the first American sheep, and thus were instrumental in developing an industry that for many years was of great importance.

It was May 21, 1851, when Amasa and Llewellyn Bixby and Dr. Thomas Flint left their Maine homes and followed the trail of the gold seekers. They sailed from New York on the steamer *Crescent City*, and met the usual conditions of travel at that period. A retelling of these facts might become monotonous; the actual experiences of each traveler were new, and varied according to the personal equipment and sensibility.

After a week the young men landed at Chagres. They started up the river on a small stern-wheel steamer, which they occupied for two days and two nights, during the latter tied up to the bank. At Gorgona they transferred to a small boat, propelled by the poles of six natives. The railroad was in course of construction, but not yet ready for use.

All the afternoon of the third day and the entire fourth was spent in a leisurely tramp over the mountain trail that led down to the western port. This walk they enjoyed greatly, observing the strange tropical land. Several times during the long day they refreshed themselves by bathing in the clear mountain pools. When from a high point of land they saw the blue Pacific, they felt like Balboa on his peak in Darian.

While waiting for the *S. S. Northerner* for San Francisco, — on which they had passage engaged — a number of days were spent happily, comfortably, and at reasonable expense in the ancient walled city of Panama.

The steamer, when it came, proved a very poor means of transportation, being much over-crowded, dirty, infested with vermin, poorly supplied with food and leaking so badly that it was necessary to use the pumps during the entire journey. A stop for a day at Acapulco brought a welcome change with dinner at a good hotel and an attractive walk into the country.

They arrived in San Francisco the sixth of July, but made no stop, going on that afternoon by boat to Sacramento, and from there on to Volcano Diggings, their objective point. Here they found Benjamin Flint, a brother of Thomas, who had come out in 1849. Their time from home was fifty-three days.

Volcano was a characteristic mining town, not far from Sutter's Mill, Mokelumne Hill, Hangtown, and other places familiar to

all who have read of those early California days. It was the point
on the overland trail to which Kit Carson was accustomed to conduct emigrants, leaving them to find their own way from there on
to their various destinations. The wheel marks of the old wagons
may still be seen on the limestone rocks above the town.

It is told that an enterprising miner from Butte City collected
enough iron tires from the wagons abandoned here to lay four
hundred feet of track in his mine.

Bayard Taylor in his charming *El Dorado* tells of a visit in '49
to this mining camp, already active and yielding rich results. Sutter
himself had been one of the first comers. Taylor suggested nearby
volcanos as the reason for the name but geological reports do not
indicate any in the neighborhood although there is igneous rock
rather generously spread about.

In the early fifties substantial buildings were put up, among
them three or more hotels. One, The National House, was built
by Dr. Flint. The St. George still stands, a three balconied ghost.
The silent almost empty town will vanish at the bottom of a lake
soon to fill the dreaming valley with the new wealth, water and the
promise of power. And travelers on the old Carson trail now the
Alpine State Highway will see no sign of Volcano, the busy little
town where my father and his brothers and cousins first lived in
California.

Llewellyn Bixby came in 1851; in 1852 his brothers, Marcellus
and Jotham, together with two cousins arrived, after a passage
around the Horn in the sailing ship, *Samuel Appleton*. Uncle Marcellus in his very terse diary commented on the monotony of the
long trip — "a dull business going to California on a sail ship."
He spoke of the beauty of the extreme southern mountains like
white marble pyramids, of the killing of an albatross with a
fourteen foot wing spread, of the cape pigeons, "the prettiest birds
alive."

The family group, numbering about a dozen, dabbled more or
less in the search for gold, but gradually turned to agricultural
pursuits. Father's mining days were limited to one week, employed
in driving a mule for gathering up pay dirt; that satisfied him. He
took a job in the local butcher shop at one hundred and fifty dollars
a month, with "keep," a very important item in those days of high
living cost. He preferred the sureness of stated wages to the uncertain promise of gold.

Apparently he and the Flints soon purchased the business and continued to conduct it as long as they remained in Volcano. They were associated in some way with Messrs. Baker and Stone, of the Buena Vista Ranch, very fertile mountain meadow land upon which heavy crops of barley were grown, and cattle were fattened for market. Another source of profit was the doctor's accurate set of apothecary scales on which he weighed gold for the miners.

After a year and a half the three of them, young men between the ages of twenty-five and thirty, determined to "unite their fortunes for the undertaking of bringing to California sheep and cattle, more for the trip than profit." Consequently, on Christmas Day, 1852, they left for home, making their way out of the mountains over roads so buried in snow as to be almost impassable. In Sacramento the river was twelve miles wide and the streets so full of water that the hack from hotel to steamer was a flat boat pulled by a horse.

In San Francisco they investigated possible ways of returning to New York. First cabin was three hundred dollars, "and get across Isthmus from Panama at your own expense." The plan adopted was to go steerage on the *S. S. Northerner*, the one upon which Dr. Flint and father had come, then unseaworthy, but now making her first trip after a thorough overhauling. The fare to Panama was only fifty dollars, which pleased their thrifty souls, and, as there were few passengers, the third-class accommodations were very comfortable, a great contrast to their previous experience. They sailed January first.

One of their problems was the safe transfer of their gold to the mint at Philadelphia. Express charges were so high they decided to avoid this expense by carrying it with them in buckskin jackets especially made for that purpose. They soon found the weight, about thirty-five hundred dollars apiece, too burdensome, so they appropriated a vacant stateroom, put the treasure between two mattresses and set a guard, one or the other of them remaining in the berth day and night.

Before leaving the steamer at Panama they packed this gold in a large chest which contained their blankets and clothing, the extra weight not being sufficient, in so large a container, to arouse suspicion, as would have been the case if they had attempted to carry it in a valise which, Dr. Flint comments, "would have had to be backed with revolver."

On landing they hired a muleteer to carry the precious box while they followed on foot, taking pains to keep the pack train in sight most of the time.

They walked as far as Cruces, spending a night on the way. They were hardly settled comfortably at the Halfway House, when there arrived a much bedraggled party, westward bound, containing women and children, whose thin-soled shoes had been little protection on the rough and muddy trail. I venture a comment that the granddaughters of these women with light shoes would have been prepared for the exigencies of such a trip with knickers and hiking boots. Those were days of gallantry, so our young men surrendered their place of shelter, and moved on in the rain to a distant shack, where, at first, there seemed no prospect of food; later, when the owner of the cabin came in, their recently acquired ability to speak Spanish stood them in good stead, and they each were favored with a cup of hot stew.

From Cruces they took a small boat down the Chagres River to Barbacoa, to which point the railroad had been completed. Here there was some delay incident to the refusal of a negro to accompany his master further on the return way to Virginia. He had discovered that by staying on the Isthmus he would escape the slavery that was his. An attempt was made to take him by force from the garret in which he had taken refuge, but was given up when the storming party, as they went up the rickety stairs of the old building, were met by the very deterring muzzles of big-bore Mexican rifles. The sympathy of the young Maine men was, naturally, with the negro. The diary comments that it was a frequent custom for Southerners to take slaves with them to do the actual work in the California gold fields.

At Aspinwall passage to New York on an independent steamer was found for twenty-five dollars, making the total fare from San Francisco but seventy-five dollars, as contrasted with three hundred dollars, the first cabin rate.

They stopped at Kingston, Jamaica, for coal. "Llewell stayed by our deposits" while the others went ashore, just as he had done at Aspinwall. I am interested to learn from these early entries that the capacity for "staying by" in times of stress was as characteristic of father in his young days as it was in later years when I knew him.

Twenty-seven days out from San Francisco they reached New York, and, taking their gold in a valise, set out at once for Philadelphia. They arrived at night and went to the Hotel Washington, where they took a room together in order to protect the valuable sachel. The next morning it was safe in the mint, where everything was assayed, fifty dollar slugs, coins from private mints of San Francisco and native gold.

Of the experience in Philadelphia, Dr. Flint writes: "January 29: Got our mint receipts of the value of our deposits. We were dressed a little rough when we arrived, and at the hotel were seated at the most inconvenient table. But as we dressed up somewhat and the report of our gold got more known we were moved pretty well up in the dining room before we left."

The next day they went on to Boston where they stopped at the United States Hotel, a hotel to which my father took me nearly forty years later, when he escorted me east to enter Wellesley College.

The evening of February first they reached their home, just a month from San Francisco. The journey west two years before had taken nearly twice as long.

Since they were among the first to return from the gold fields, they were objects of great interest to all the neighbors round about. They had scores of visitors, all eager for news of their own men-folk in far-away California, the land so vaguely known, its great distances so under-estimated. They assumed that the returned travelers might know everyone in the new state.

They visited at home for five weeks. "We talked," says Dr. Flint, "until our vocal cords could stand the strain no longer and were glad to start west."

CHAPTER V

Driving Sheep Across The Plains

O N March 8, 1853, the cousins began the long return journey by rail, horseback, emigrant wagon and foot that ended just ten months later at San Gabriel, in Southern California. Dr. Flint, at the end of his diary, sums up the distances as follows:

"Today closes the year 1853, and one year from the time we left San Francisco on the *S. S. Northerner;* in which time we have traveled by steamship 5,344 miles. By railroad 2,144 miles. I have, by steamboat on Mississippi and Missouri Rivers, 1,074 miles. On horseback and on foot 2,131 miles, making a total of 10,693 on a direct line between points reached."

This diary is said to have especial historical value because the author put down daily specific facts of cost, distance and conditions of travel. Many accounts of the overland trip are but memories.

As I have read the journal I have been impressed with the idea that while it took vision, health and character on the part of the young pioneers to accomplish their object, the burdens came only day by day and would not be refused by the vigorous young grandsons whom I know now, were the same rewards offered for enterprise and endurance.

The railroad journey from Boston to Terre Haute, the western terminus of the road, was a very different one from that of today, taking then a week instead of a few hours.

They went down from Anson and Norridgwock to Boston where they exchanged their "money at Suffolk Bank for their bills, as they were good anywhere West, and none others were."

Leaving Boston at 8 a.m., an all day ride took them to Albany, where they spent the night at the Delavan House. They went on early the next morning to Buffalo, which was reached at 11 p.m. Here they "put up at the Clarendon House. Tired. Sleepy." At eleven in the forenoon they left for Cincinnati, reaching Cleveland at 8 p.m., Columbus at 4 a.m., where they changed cars, and arrived at their destination late at night, after a thirty-six hour ride in day coaches. They rested at Cincinnati until the next afternoon, when they went over to Dayton for the purpose of making an early start on the last lap of the railroading. The entry for March 16 reads:

"Called at 2 o'clock a.m., went aboard cars at 2½. No breakfast, nor could we get a mouthful until we arrived in Indianapolis, at 2½ o'clock p.m. The R. R. was new, rough and no stations by the way. Arrived in Terre Haute about 5 p.m.

Here they stopped for a week at the Prairie House. They organized their firm of Flint, Bixby & Co., in which Benjamin, who had been longer in California, had four parts to three each for the others. They wrote letters, bought three horses, fitted saddles to them, and, on March 19th, started west for Paris, Illinois, over "roads as bad as mud can make them."

They went across the state, a few miles a day, calling occasionally on an old friend or on one of their many cousins who had settled in the Middle West. Once they stopped over night in Urbana at the Middlesex House, where they found six beds in a 6x9 room, and had for breakfast "fried eggs swimming in lard, the almost universal food in this part of the world."

By April first they had arrived in Quincy. "Had a hard time finding the town," says Dr. Flint. "Most of the way through oak-wooded prairie, uncultivated. . . Horseback distance from Terre Haute, 348 miles."

Quincy was their headquarters while they were seeking and buying sheep, finding a few at one place, a few at another. Father once told me of the vexations they had at first, trying to drive in one homogeneous band all these little groups of sheep, each with its own bell wether.

During the last of April and the first of May, while still buying stock, they sheared their sheep at Warsaw, Illinois, selling the wool, 6,410 pounds, for $1,570.45 to Connable-Smith Co., of Keokuk, Iowa. At this time it is recorded that father received a remittance of $1,000 from a California acquaintance, undoubtedly a welcome addition to their funds with such an undertaking ahead of them. They must have had their trip well planned before they left Volcano, for Pacific Coast mail to meet them thus.

On May 7 they started off for the overland journey with 1,880 sheep, young and old, eleven yoke of oxen, two cows, four horses, two wagons, complete camping outfit, four men, three dogs, and themselves. They ferried across the Mississippi River at Keokuk for sixty-two dollars.

At some time during the trip the number of sheep was increased, for I have always heard it said that the flock contained 2,400, and I have a later brief resume of the trip, made by Dr. Flint, in which he mentions the larger number.

There was much travel across the plains at this time. The entry for May 8 is: "In Keokuk. Visited the Mormon camp where it was said there were 3,400 proselytes from Europe, 278 emigrant wagons ready to convey them to Salt Lake. A motley crowd of English, Welsh, Danes, etc."

Father and Ben went on across Iowa with their train, while Dr. Flint went alone by steamer to St. Louis to purchase further supplies, which he took up the Missouri on the *S. S. El Paso* to meet his partners at Council Bluffs.

It is interesting to note that while he was in St. Louis he heard Prof. Agassiz lecture on geology. St. Louis was a far cry from Cambridge, but in this golden age of American lectures men took long and hard trips to carry knowledge to eager learners. How fortunate that Mr. Bryan had not yet arisen to combat the spread of scientific thinking!

The trip up the river from St. Louis to Council Bluffs took ten days, due in part to the many stops for loading and unloading, and to the necessity for tying up at night because of changing currents and shifting banks. There is mention of frontier settlements, of Indians along shore and of the varied passengers, among them a group of fourteen Baptist ministers, going to attend a convention. Their presence brought about the curious anomaly of "prayer meeting at one end of the saloon, cards at the other." By Sunday, the 29th, the preachers had disembarked, and the steamer was "getting above moral and religious influences as we leave civilization behind and touch the wild and woolly west."

The steamer arrived at Kanesville (Council Bluffs) on May 30, where the supplies were landed during a severe storm. The place was a "town of huts, and full of sharp dealers who live off the emigrants . . . the outpost of the white man."

Here Dr. Flint met Ben and Llewell with their sheep and wagons, but the crossing of the river was delayed for a week by the heavy rains.

After a final gathering of supplies, the purchase of an additional saddle horse and another wagon, the stock was ferried across the Missouri River and they found themselves "fairly on the plains."

The personnel of the party varied from time to time. Dr. Flint says there were fifteen men, but does not name them all. Three men, after a couple of weeks, became faint-hearted and turned back. The teamsters, Jennings, who served also as butcher, White, the carpenter, and John Trost, the "Dutchman," appear to have made the entire trip with them.

There is frequent mention of William C. Johnson, who, with his bride Mary, left the party with which they had been traveling and added their wagon to ours. Mrs. Johnson, the only woman in the train, contributed to the general comfort by baking bread for them all, and on gala days making apple pie or doughnuts.

This comparatively small group of men and wagons, with much stock, made conditions somewhat different from those recently pictured in *The Covered Wagon,* and yet this film has made real to many the hazards and fatigue, the courage and the heartbreak, the manner of life and travel that were common to all who crossed the plains. The route chosen by my people differed from that pictured in that it lay altogether north of the Platte River.

From the first of June until the middle of July they were on the prairies; from then on they were in the Rocky Mountains until the first of September, when they came down into the Valley of the Great Salt Lake. By the first of October they were well under way again, following the Fremont Trail to San Bernardino, a journey of three months. I have given a brief report of their route; the diary is full of interesting details of daily happenings, of the type of country through which they passed, of the things that grew by the wayside and of the various animals they encountered. Comments on the landscape give a hint of the love of beauty in the writer, but, being a New Englander, he does not indulge in much emotional or florid language.

I was interested in several mentions of the guide-book, Horne's, which evidently mapped out the routes with more or less detail. Sometimes they found the statements accurate, sometimes not.

The sending of a letter home from time to time makes one realize that the trail, though long and hard, was a traveled one, and that they were not entirely isolated. Occasionally they were overtaken and passed by those who could go more rapidly, unhampered by the slow-moving sheep. Father often said that he walked across the continent; he had a saddle horse, Nig, but, going at a sheep's pace, he found it pleasanter on foot.

When they started out from Council Bluffs they met reports that Indians ahead were troublesome, but they did not encounter any for nearly a month. Then one day a couple of Omahas, carrying an English musket, old style, were in camp for a time. Probably it was one of these who two days later tried to steal Dr. Flint's horse, and, discovered, killed James Force who was standing guard. The nature of the bullet wound indicated the musket. Father told me it was his regular watch, but this man had taken it that fatal night, in return for some favor father had shown him.

The last of July they had a second meeting with Indians, but fortunately without casualties on either side. Dr. Flint says: "Soon after halting, an half dozen Indians bounded out of the brush and commenced to pillage the wagons. The teamsters, Johnson, Palmer, and Jennings, were scared out of their wits and offered no resistance, but Mrs. Johnson went after their hands with a hatchet when they went to help themselves to things in her wagon. . . Two more Indians joined those already present, — one of them with a certificate that they were Good Indians. It was written in faultless penmanship, expressing the hope we would treat them well, so we gave them some hard tack and a sheep that was lame. . . The Indians were greatly astonished when they found that we could use the Spanish language. We found that they were a hunting and marauding party of Arapahoes from Texas."

Shortly after this our party overtook a desolate train of Mormons, — mostly women and children from England, — who had been robbed of all their provisions by these "Good Indians," and who would have perished but for the timely arrival of our people, who supplied them with sufficient food to carry them through to their destination.

By the middle of August the company crossed South Pass and "drank from Pacific Springs." They went past Fort Bridger, where they left the Oregon Trail and turned southward through the mountains into Utah. As they were going down the last defiles into the broad valley they were met by watchers who enquired if they were saints or sinners. When it was known that they were the people who were the saviors of the robbed and stranded Mormons, they were given a royal welcome by Brigham Young and his saints. Their flocks were turned into the Church pastures, and they were given free access to the gardens. After long months of camp fare they enjoyed greatly the plenty of this promised land, the green corn, squashes, potatoes and melons.

It had been their intent to drive their stock directly across Nevada and the Sierras into Central California, their destination, but the season was so late they feared the heavy snows that were imminent in the high mountains. They therefore determined to travel southwest into Southern California and from there to drive up the coast.

After about three weeks of rest and recuperation, with flocks augmented by purchase from the Mormons, they set out upon the hardest portion of the trail.

From this time on there is frequent mention of other parties engaged in similar enterprise. A number of these joined forces for mutual protection against the Indians, who were very troublesome in the Southwest. They attempted to stampede the horses and cattle, which were easily frightened. The sheep were not so hard to protect, for they when alarmed huddled closer to the camp fire.

Although the men were constantly annoyed by the attempts of the Indians to run off stock, they managed to avoid actual conflict and no lives were lost.

When the Indians did succeed in cutting out some of the stock they would return it, on being paid at the rate of two "hickory" shirts (the khaki of that day) for a cow, and one for a calf. On one occasion the Indians brought in venison for sale, which was bought and eaten, before it was discovered that the number of "deer" corresponded exactly with the number of colts that were missing.

Anyone who has made the rail trip between Salt Lake City and Los Angeles can appreciate the references made in the diary to the rough and stony trails, the dust, the days without water or food for the animals, to sage-brush and cactus, and can but wonder how it was possible to get flocks across the desert country at all.

On the earlier part of this trail, where there was still some noticeable vegetation, they lost many sheep through the eating of poison weeds. They lost others through the drinking of poor water or the entire lack of it for many weary miles.

At one place they had trouble with quicksands, at another the sheep balked at crossing the Rio Virgin and father and two helpers spent a whole afternoon packing on their backs one sheep at a time across the hundred-foot ford.

On the third of December, the Flint-Bixby train and the Hollister train started together on the hardest portion of the whole trip — about a hundred miles without water, except for the meager Bitter Water Springs. Most of the wagons and the cattle went on ahead, and after three days reached the Springs, where they waited for the other men with the sheep. On the fourth day the first of the

Hollister sheep came in; on the fifth, in the morning, came Ben and father, and in the afternoon Hub Hollister. Dr. Flint mentions the oxen as being "famished for want of food and particularly for water, a sad sight of brute suffering." With the arrival of the sheep, the cattle again went on to the Mojave River. The sheep did not arrive until the fourteenth, after eleven days spent in crossing the desert. The diary tells something of the trouble experienced. Dr. Flint says: "I packed my horse with provisions and started back to meet Ben and Llewell with the sheep. Met them some six miles out. They had used up all their water and food, hence it was a relief to them when I hove in sight. Some of the men had such a dread of the desert that they were beside themselves, imagining they would perish from thirst before getting over the forty miles." It appears from this that the prime movers in the enterprise must not only be brave and fearless themselves, but must also provide courage for their helpers.

It was this stretch of desert that caused the greatest loss to men who imported sheep in this manner. Just how many of ours died, or had to be abandoned, I have never heard, but my father told me that they were fortunate in losing fewer than the average.

After reaching the Mojave River they all rested for several days, "the men loafing about the camps for pitching horse shoes." Evidently this favorite masculine sport did not defer its entry into California until the arrival of the Iowa contingent.

Conditions at last were better. They camped on dry burr clover instead of sand and stones and "had a big fire of cottonwood, which gave a cosy look to the camp." They had a stew of wild ducks and got "a mess of quail for Christmas dinner on the morrow."

On the 29th they "moved on towards the summit of the Sierras. Warm and pleasant. Green grass in places two inches high. Snow clad mountains on our right."

On Friday the 30th they crossed the mountains through Cajon Pass, and on New Year's Day, the scribe to whom we are indebted for the detailed account of this long journey was the guest of the Hollisters at San Bernardino for dinner. Father told me they celebrated by having doughnuts. It is evident that the two trains came in together, sometimes one ahead, sometimes the other. I make note of the fact of their traveling in company because I have seen it stated in print that Col. Hollister was the first to bring American sheep to California. I am pleased to be able to offer this contemporary witness to the fact that there are others to share the honor.

Mention is made of the sheep of Frazer, White and Viles and McClanahan as well as of Col. Hollister and Flint, Bixby & Co., all of whom shared the hardships of the trail those last days of 1853.

The San Bernardino into which they came after their long trip across the desert was a Mormon colony which had been founded three years earlier.

After spending the New Year at San Bernardino the herds that we have followed across the plains moved on to the "Coco Mongo" (Cucamunga) ranch and vineyard.

This was apparently a current spelling as it occurs in official government documents. It is a word of Indian origin meaning a sandy place. The first grapevines which still surprise the passer-by with their growth in seemingly pure sand had been planted some ten years before this. The old winery stands just north of the Foothill Boulevard between Upland and Cucamonga.

The next drive took the men and sheep across the valley to the Williams Ranch, the Santa Ana del Chino, and after a night there they moved on to San Gabriel, which they reached the evening of January seventh. The entry of the journal for January ninth would indicate that new comers seventy years ago were as impressed by orange trees as are the tourists of today: — "A beautiful scene at sunrise. There had been a light flurry of snow during the night which stuck to the orange leaves and to the fruit, which, when lighted by the clear morning sun made a most beautiful contrast of colors tropical and arctic."

On that date they moved over to the ranges of the Rancho San Pasqual where they had been able to rent pasturage. This is the site of the present city of Pasadena. Here they camped for the remainder of the winter.

"The only incident out of the ordinary routine of camp life for two months," says Dr. Flint, "was the birth of a son to Mr. and Mrs. Johnson."

In the spring they moved northward, through Ventura and Santa Barbara; thence through the mountains to Paso Robles and San Luis Obispo, again over the high hills and onward until they came to San Jose, where they rented the Rancho Santa Teresa and pastured their sheep for fourteen months. They sheared and sold their wool to Moore and Folger, familiar names in those old days. They sold wethers for mutton at $16.00 a head and bought a thousand sheep at $5.00. Then in the summer of 1855 they moved to Monterey County in search of feed, and, in October, bought from Francisco Perez Pacheco the Rancho San Justo, half of which they soon sold to their friend Col. Hollister.

With the purchase of this first land, Flint, Bixby & Co. were definitely located and for forty years San Juan Bautista was their headquarters. After father's death the firm was dissolved and the properties separated, the Flints retaining the lands in the north and the Bixby heirs those in Southern California.

CHAPTER VI

Rancho San Justo

RANCHO San Justo is beautiful for location. Its rolling fields and oak-dotted hills are framed by the mountains that close the southern end of the valley of Santa Clara and San Jose. The wide acres lying adjacent to San Juan Bautista must once have been a part of the mission holdings, lost at the time of disestablishment.

Over the hills from Salinas and Monterey came El Camino Real, trodden in Mexican and Spanish days by priest and soldier and rare wayfarer. The mission founded in 1797 was one of the finest. It was famous for its nine bells, the tiny box organ used to win the Indians, and the chorals and hymns composed by Father Estaban Tapis. He wrote on parchment bold notes whose value was indicated not only by position but also by colors varied for different tones. The little organ and three of the books may still be seen at the mission.

The plaza in San Juan has suffered less change than almost any other in California. In addition to the mission is an old adobe inn and the balconied, tree-shaded house of General José Castro. This town became the home of the young men we have followed across the plains, and for all their later business lives was the background of their picture.

It is hard to visualize the emptiness during the fifties of the outlying territory. The vast stretches of open valley and hill land were practically uninhabited and were infested with wild beasts, and sometimes wilder men. A very vivid impression of this may be obtained by anyone fortunate enough to read an account of "A Dangerous Journey from San Francisco to San Luis Obispo," given by J. Ross Browne in his book called *Crusoe's Island*. He spent one of his nights in the San Juan Inn, a place he found very gruesome because of the whispers of the desperation to which the woman in charge had been driven during the terrible privations and tragedy of her overland trip. Another transient guest at this same inn was Bayard Taylor who tells in his delightful *El Dorado* of a night here during a walk from San Francisco to Monterey.

The earliest records of our life at San Justo I have found in a series of letters written during the summer of 1857 by my father's sister, Nancy Dinsmore Bixby. She and Ann Flint, sister of Thomas and Benjamin, came out, bringing with them from Maine credentials testifying to their ability as teachers. Whether or not they did teach in California I do not know. Nancy later married here Mr. William E. Lovett of Monterey. Ann remained at the ranch for several years and then returned to Maine, where she married Mr. C. D. Nichols.

The first letter of June fifth was written from the Howard House in New York City where Ann and Nancy, Dr. Thomas and Benjamin with their brides, Henry and Flint Bixby and George Moore were gathered preparatory for sailing the next day for California, on *S. S. Illinois.* It is not clear whether or not the last two named were coming or going, but they were associated in business during these years with Augustus Rufus Bixby near Paso Robles. In the second letter, written "on board the *Sonora* somewhere in the Pacific," Nancy tells of the varied experiences of the trip made familiar to us from many letters and diaries of the period now in print. The added ease and quickness of crossing the Isthmus that had come during the six years since Dr. Flint's first trip is noticeable. The railroad had been completed. The ship docked at San Francisco June thirtieth, twenty-four days from New York. The travelers were met by father who appears to have stayed at the ranch while the first delegation went back to New England to marry.

The venture of bringing sheep across the plains had proved good and a wide estate had been acquired. What more natural than for the young men to think of home-building, which is in a primary way state-building. Not content with the women the west at that time afforded, each in his turn, like that ancient sheep-man, Jacob, made a pilgrimage back to the land from which he came in search of a wife of his own people; but, unlike the old patriarch, it did not take them long to find the bride willing to return to that far-off glamorous California.

Benjamin Flint married at six o'clock of a June morning Caroline Lavina Getchell, a girl from his old home town of Anson. As soon as the ceremony was over, amid both smiles and tears, they started for the distant ranch, by way of Portland, Boston, New York and Panama. Up in Woodstock, Vermont, his brother Thomas had married Mary Mitchell and they also journeyed to New York to sail on the same steamer with Ben and Caddie. Marcellus Bixby they left behind in Norridgewock but it was only a few months before he followed in their footsteps, bringing back to San Juan his bride, Amanda Gould.

During this marrying summer father stayed in charge at the San Justo and Jotham at the Buena Vista, which belonged to him and Marcellus. Before the latter returned with his wife the ranch was sold. A little later they invested the proceeds in fifteen hundred sheep which they kept on range near San Miguel, making their home, however, in San Juan Bautista. Amanda wrote home that they had a very convenient house for California. They bought their furniture in San Jose and had "everything to make them comfortable and in much better style than she had expected." Dr. Edward Bixby of San Francisco and Mr. Herbert Bixby of Buena Park are sons of this couple. Aunt Amanda died while her boys were still small and later Uncle Marcellus married Adelaide C. Foster, the aunt of that family whom I knew.

Father's marriage did not follow until two years after these others. At Bloomfield, Maine, in April 1859, he married my mother's oldest sister, Sarah Hathaway, — but more of this later.

After this long digression let us turn back to the group we left standing on the dock at San Francisco. According to Nancy's third letter they stayed in the city at the International Hotel for a couple of days, seeing the sights and meeting a number of old friends who had preceded them to California.

The early morning of the third day marked the beginning of the last lap of the long journey. They went down the beautiful bay on a small steamer a distance of twelve miles where they met the San Jose stage. This took them so swiftly over the smooth straight road that they reached this, the oldest pueblo of the state, for supper.

It was the first sight of the strange dry country for the four girls. For May, Caddie and Nancy it was to be their permanent home, for Ann a stay of five or six years. They had come from the lush greenness of New England in June. Here they saw great fields of ripened grain, interspersed with long stretches of yellow mustard, ten feet tall, Nancy wrote. Very likely it was. I myself remember a growth luxurious far beyond any I now see. The trees she noticed were occasional live oaks hung with mistletoe.

The first day's journey ended at nightfall in San Jose, where they remained for three days. They called on friends, saw a French garden, whatever that may have been, and drove under the oaks and cottonwoods that shaded the Alameda. At the end of this drive they found Mrs. Simons with her little two-year-old Mollie, so loved in later years as Mrs. Frank Gibson, and week-old Carrie, her keen and able sister, Mrs. Greene.

On Sunday they attended the Presbyterian meeting and tried to go to Catholic service but there was none that day. They were however welcomed by a sister who graciously admitted them to "a female seminary" connected with the mission and showed them the gardens and school rooms and treasures of paintings and embroideries.

Early Monday morning they started on again and drove the forty-five miles to the ranch, which they reached that same night.

The first home of our young folk, on the eastern side of San Justo, consisted of four houses and a shed which had been put together. Nancy says: "I don't know what kind of a looking place this is in the winter, but it looks as dry and barren now as a desert." However they seemed to be very comfortable and happy there. They had a sitting room, four bedrooms, a dining room, a stove room, but not enough closets. "They are thinking of hauling up another house as we have not quite room enough." There is no indication of the source of these houses so available for addition. When they arrived they found Nick keeping houses, with everything neat as a pin. I don't know who Nick may have been but he seems to have been a valuable person.

Across the valley about five miles away was the home of Col. Hollister and his sister Aunty Brown. Over there was a good house, the little lake, and gardens from which our household was able to get all kinds of fresh vegetables and fruit. There was frequent friendly visiting back and forth, and finally an exchange of properties. The Hollisters sold their half and the city of Hollister was founded upon it.

Nancy was delighted, on her first call upon Mrs. Brown, to see the pond, the first fresh water she had seen in California. Like others who come here she comments that all our rivers are dry. Their only other neighbors were the Burnaps. Mr. Burnap made many cheeses, and "we have his cheese but it doesn't taste like mother's." The girls did the housework which was "not enough to keep me from growing lazy . . . we have to cook enough for us to eat and keep our house swept and the boys don't have any more to do than we; all they do is to milk the cows and bring in the

water." Nancy, however, made the butter. And they did their washing, taking it to Mrs. Brown's, for their own water was so bad "it
couldn't be used without breaking."

Apparently this first home was something of a picnic for these
pioneers, still young enough to be boys and girls together. They had
a good time, and were glad that their isolation allowed "as much
noise as we please without rousing the neighbors, which I esteem a
great privilege."

The last letter written in September was a long one and tells a
different story. Sheep-shearing was on and that meant hard work
for everybody.

"We have twenty-nine in our family," she writes, "and cook meat
three times a day for them." One of the girls was sick so the other
three did the work. It is interesting to note that it was well organized with individual assignments and times for rest. For example,
May who washed up the breakfast dishes and got dinner did not
have to get up in the morning until nine o'clock.

They were shearing at the rate of four hundred sheep a day and
at the time of the letter there were sixty of the great wool sacks
stuffed ready for shipment.

There is sometimes an interest in prices. Nancy bought a good
pair of boots for two dollars. Ann got calico for a dress at fourteen
cents a yard, and for a comforter for eleven cents, "almost as cheap
as at home."

There are no more letters from Nancy, but three years later one
went from Aunt Sarah, father's young wife, to his mother, telling
of the birth of Nancy's first son. She had married William Edward
Lovett from Monterey and they were living in San Juan. Children
had come to the others, also, — to the doctor and May, to Benjamin
and Caddie, to Marcellus and Amanda. None ever came to Llewellyn and Sarah, a great disappointment.

Nancy had other children, two more sons and two daughters. As
I have learned more of her I have felt a growing kinship with her.
She wrote verses of a type similar to mine. The one most familiar
to us gives memories of her childhood in Maine, just as I write of
my childhood in California. Her daughter told me of her writing
this particular poem while she was going about her work, carrying
paper and pencil in her apron pocket, and taking it out in the midst
of baking to add a line or two. Recently I saw a portrait she had
made, exquisitely drawn in crayon. Making of portraits is an avoca-
tion of mine. Apparently some of the same *genes* fell to our lot.

Father's marriage to Sarah Hathaway started the series of Hathaway-Bixby marriages. The way of it was this. Soon after his return to Norridgewock, he, with many others, was a guest at the annual church party at the home of Mr. Hathaway, the minister of the parish at Bloomfield. He had been told that he would find "a passel" of pretty girls there, and was advised that Margaret, the second, was especially beautiful. That was a fateful party! Out of it came the destiny of all the five daughters, — the four who married Bixby's and the fifth who became foster mother to three of us children.

It was not the recommended, witty, black-eyed Margaret, however, who won the love of Llewellyn, but the oldest girl, tall, blue-eyed Sarah, whose name I bear. She captured his heart, and soon left Maine to go with him the long way, by Panama, to the distant ranch of San Justo.

What more natural than that when, shortly, brother Jotham returned to his home, he should go over to the neighboring parsonage to bear the greetings of his sister-in-law, Sarah, to her family? It is told that, when upon this errand he met at the gate the lovely Margaret, he lost his heart completely. He never regained it. When he was eighty he told me emphatically that his wife not only had been the most beautiful woman in California, but that she still was.

A few months after this meeting Margaret traveled with friends across the Isthmus, and up the coast to San Francisco, there to be met by her sister and taken to the ranch to await her marriage day, which came quickly. She was married in her own new home in San Juan by the minister, Dr. Edwards, who had recently been a missionary among the Chocktaw Indians. A letter describing the ceremony tells of the usual preparations, the making of bride's cake and wedding cake, of putting the finishing touches on the little house, of the arranging of the wedding veil and the gathering in the early evening of the group of friends and relatives, including three little folks that had already come into the different families.

The home began immediately, and a few days later a call at the house discovered the bride happy in her housework and doing the first family washing.

This wedding ceremony was the first that Dr. Edwards had ever performed for white people, but it is reported to have been so well done that no one would have guessed inexperience. It is to be hoped that his later services in this line were as successful as this one. He was still the minister in San Juan when I was a child and he was wont to entertain me by repeating the Lord's Prayer in Choctaw.

The same letter which reports the marriage speaks of the new ranch house that was building and of the hope that it would be ready for occupancy in about two months, which dates the building for me, — early in 1863.

It was in 1861 that the exchange had been made with the Hollisters. At first our people lived in the house already there, which must have been the one that was used in my childhood for the hired men. It was inadequate for the needs of the three families, to whom children were coming, so a larger home was necessary. The men were intimate and congenial, and dreamed of an enlargement and continuation of their associated lives; the income was ample so they proceeded to build them a great house, a communal house, a staunch Maine house, white-painted and green-shuttered, as solid and true today as sixty years ago,—but, alas, now idle.* This was the house in which I was born.

They planted the garden about it and the orchard, beside the pond where the hills could look to see if their trees were on straight. In wintertime those hills were as green as any of Maine in June, but in our rainless summer they were soft tan or gold against the cobalt sky.

To accommodate three families there were three apartments, each with sitting-room, bedroom and bath, and in addition, for the use of the whole group, a common parlor, large office, dining room, and kitchen, together with numerous guest rooms in the upper story. Every convenience of the period was included, — ample closets, modern plumbing, sufficient fireplaces.

The plan for housekeeping in this large establishment was for each wife in turn to take charge for a month. It was no small undertaking to provide for the household, with the growing flocks of children and the frequent addition of visiting sisters, cousins, or aunts. The women involved, being individuals, had differing capacities and ideas, and each had the desire for a home managed according to her own idea. Imagine sitting down to every meal with six parents, twelve children and half a dozen guests! Inevitably the communal plan could not but fail to be altogether ideal. For a wonder it held together in a fashion for fifteen years, but there were many trips to San Francisco to relieve the strain, or long visits of mothers and children in Maine, that I guess might not have been

---

*Note, 1931. This is now the property of Walter Hedges, Jr., and the house has been incorporated in the development of a large country estate.

so frequent or of so long duration if there had been individual homes for the cousin-partners. Ultimately the Ben Flints took up a permanent residence in Oakland and we moved to Los Angeles, leaving the Dr. Flints on the ranch.

However, San Juan remained the center of business operations so long as the firm lasted. During the earlier years a large business was built and many and varied affairs instituted.

It was not long after the purchase of the San Justo before the flocks increased beyond the capacity of the original ranch to support them, and since the wool business was very profitable other lands were bought. As a little girl I used to hear of necessary trips to the "Worry Worry" ranch. Those were the very trying years of the great depression of the seventies and I suppose it relieved father's feelings to pronounce Huer-Huero in this fashion.

This ranch was in San Luis Obispo County in the region of Paso Robles. The original grantee of the land was José Mariano Bonilla and the grant comprised three leagues, about fifteen thousand six hundred acres. I have not found just when or how Flint, Bixby & Company acquired it. To this they added over thirty-one thousand acres of government land. The ranch was sold intact about 1880. The purchasers cut it into smaller parcels, and much of it has been developed as farming and fruit land. Our business belonged to the pastoral age of California. Our successors introduced the agricultural.

None of the family ever lived at the Huer-Huero. It was directed from San Justo and was under the immediate care of a foreman.

The firm first entered Los Angeles County in 1866, with the purchase from John Temple of Rancho Los Cerritos. Later, with Jotham Bixby, they bought seventeen thousand acres of the Rancho Palos Verdes, which they sold in 1915 to Mr. Vanderlip. The beautiful community now developing on the estate satisfies an old dream.

At one time Flint, Bixby & Company were half owners of the great San Joaquin Ranch in Orange County. They sold their interest to James Irvine, owner of the other half. They held also a sixth share in the Alamitos Ranch.

The large acreages were acquired when people in California were few and far between and when the land was considered fit only for grazing. As settlers came in it was sold in comparatively large parcels to men with sufficient capital to subdivide and sell as small farms or town lots.

While the first interest of this firm of vigorous young men was stock-raising, before long it branched out in several directions. The idea of profiting from Captain Cook's goats was undoubtedly related to wool-gathering! It seems that on Guadeloupe Island, off the coast of Lower California, there were some thirty thousand wild goats, descendents, tradition says, from a few left by the famous captain.

The bright idea of F., B. & Co. was that by the introduction of high-grade Angora goats the quality of the pelts might be so improved as to give them commercial value. And so a concession from the Mexican government was secured and experiments were begun. When Thomas Flint, Jr., visited the island in 1874 they had on hand fifteen hundred white half-breeds. The original goats were black. Several shipments of pelts were made but the enterprise was abandoned before they could carry out all their plans. I am told that within recent years new dreamers have made similar ventures, with similar results.

Guadaloupe Island is one of the few remaining haunts of the strange sea-elephant. The island itself is barren and uninteresting. The goats have wrecked both themselves and the vegetation, all of which they have devoured. I am glad we are not responsible for the introduction of the original wreckers. The fact that we turned some of them white probably did not make them any hungrier.

The name of this firm became well known in staging history of the west. In 1869 they bought the Coast Line Stage Company from William E. Lovett who had started it a year or two earlier. At first it operated from San Jose south to Los Angeles and San Diego, but very shortly they disposed of their interests between the latter two places. For several years they held an important place in the transportation of passengers, mail and Wells Fargo express, but as the railroad made extensions the courses of the stage were gradually shortened.

When the Southern Pacific pierced the mountains near San Fernando and completed the rail connection between San Francisco and Los Angeles by way of the San Joaquin Valley, and joined Santa Barbara and Los Angeles in similar fashion, the day of the stages was practically over. The company retained and operated until nearly 1890 the short stretch from Santa Barbara over the hills to Santa Inez. This section was continued until the railroad made its way through the mountains at Point Conception and completed the coast road to San Francisco.

One of my pleasant memories is of a visit to Santa Barbara with my father in 1889 when we went on a tour of inspection over the last bit of stage road. We went to the summit of San Marcos Pass. The wife of the station-keeper made a gala occasion of our luncheon for which she prepared food that she remembered to be much liked by father. It must have been a sort of farewell-to-staging feast.

The route of the Coast Line Stage Company was very much that of the Coast Highway so familiar to present day motorists. It was our company that built the San Juan Grade, rebuilt the Cuesta Pass road, and built that through San Marcos Pass. The latter was a toll road, later bought by Santa Barbara County. The old stage station at the northern foot of this road still stands. We also constructed the road through the Conejo.

Between Santa Barbara and Ventura the stages followed the beach, an uncertain and dangerous road now protected by the miles of causeway. I do not know whether or not a stage ever met disaster here, but not long ago Senator del Valle told me of a mishap that did occur. Señor Ulpiano Yndart was en route with his family and treasures from Santa Barbara to Rancho Los Cerritos where he had accepted a position as manager for John Temple, when, rounding Punta Gordo on the beach, an unexpected great wave came up out of the sea and stole a chest containing jewels and heirlooms that had come to him from an early sea captain member of the family.

Some years later Señora Yndart was ill and, realizing that she could not live long, sent for Señora del Valle, mother of Senator del Valle. She gave into her care a little daughter, together with one of the treasure chests that escaped the waves, to serve as dowry when the child should be grown and married. The acceptance of the trust was in line with the generous and sympathetic custom of the early Californians, and the reward came in the love and devotion of the foster daughter.

When the stages were first started the schedule called for three trips a week, but soon the amount of travel demanded a daily coach. The time from Los Angeles to San Francisco by stage and train was sixty-six hours. The fare from Los Angeles to San Jose where the train connection was made was twenty-five dollars, with stop-over privileges.

The stages used were of the popular Concord make. They played their part in the romantic period of the earlier American day in California. Their coming and going through the small towns lent interest and excitement, with dashing six-horse teams, with news and passengers and perhaps an account of bandits and holdups. Now they belong to museums, movies, pageants, fiestas, or may be had in replica to adorn a mantel shelf.

The making of beet sugar also engaged the interest of this group of enterprising young men. They, with several other firms organized and built at Alvarado, Alameda County, the first successful beet sugar factory not only in California, but in the United States. The initial run was in 1870. They transferred a little later their interest to a second factory in Soquel in Santa Cruz County.

This new industry suffered from drought, insect pests, price-cutting by competing cane sugar interests and from the fact that at that time the process of making sugar from beets had not been developed to the point it now is and that consequently the product was not popular. In 1880 the Soquel factory was closed.

Father, however, retained a belief in the ultimate practicability of sugar-making in California, and his last business undertaking was an attempt to re-establish it on the Cerritos, near Long Beach. It was in 1896, the year of the free silver agitation, and he was unable to finance a sugar factory himself. He therefore induced the Clark interests to buy some of our land, build the sugar factory at Los Alamitos, and give us a preference in the raising of beets.

This was the year of my father's death. Uncle Ben had died in 1882, Dr. Flint went in 1904, and the adventures and pioneering work of the cousins became a part of history.

CHAPTER VII

Los Alamitos and Los Cerritos

F O R many reasons our choice of Los Angeles as a residence was a
very happy one. In the first place it gave my father an opportunity to keep in touch with his business interests in the southern
part of the state, and in the second it fulfilled two dear wishes of
my mother.

It had been her desire for years to get away from the large ranch
house at San Justo, with its crowds of people, and into a small home
of her own where she could surround her children with influences
and conditions that accorded with her ideals.

Again, it was joy to her to be near her two sisters, who lived on
the neighboring ranches, Los Cerritos and Los Alamitos, and her
father who had recently come to Southern California.

The three families were doubly related, — Hathaway mothers
and Bixby fathers, Mary and Llewellyn, Margaret and Jotham,
Susan and John. I have told of my father's marriage to Sarah
Hathaway. She was always a delicate girl and lived only six years
after she came west as a bride. There were no children, much to
the disappointment of them both. After an interval of six years
father returned to Maine and married my mother, Mary, the little
sister of his loved Sarah, who had, in the twelve years passed, grown
to womanhood. When I came I was given the name of this beloved
older sister and wife.

Before this time Jotham Bixby and his family had moved from
San Juan to the Cerritos Ranch, bringing with them for company
at the isolated home, his wife's sister Susan, who in the course of
time married the young cousin, John W. Bixby, newly come from
Maine.

He was a son of Simon Bixby and Deborah Flint, a sister of
William Flint, the father of Benjamin and Thomas. Several of
his older brothers were in California at the time, and his sister
Eulalia Bixby was one of the earliest public school teachers in Los
Angeles. He had been a teacher himself in Maine before he came

west, although he was not more than twenty-two or three. Like young men of today going into a new country he looked for a job, and was ready to turn his hand to anything that offered. He soon found a place with his cousin, Jotham, at the Cerritos, learning ranching, doing carpentering, using his skill with tools in the making of cabinets and bookcases that are still in use. He was a very useful ranch man during the day, a welcome member of the family during the evening. He was tall, handsome, full of fun, and musical. His later life proved him a wise and successful business man and a public spirited citizen.

John and Susan fell in love and became engaged and kept their secret right under the noses of interested friends and relatives who were planning all sorts of matrimonial alliances except the one that was planning itself — one destined to exceptional happiness.

When they married they left the Cerritos and lived in Wilmington, where they remained for several years. They moved their home to the Alamitos about the time that we came south to settle in Los Angeles.

The intimate connection of double blood-kinship and of business association made the three families seem like one and us children like brothers and sisters.

Our home in Los Angeles became the headquarters for the out-of-town relatives, and several times a week we had some of them for luncheon guests. On the other hand we of the town grasped every chance to spend a day, a week, or the long summer vacation at one of the adobes. All the festival days were shared. Cerritos claimed the Fourth of July most often, for its bare courtyard offered a spot free from fire hazard. What a satisfying supply of fire-works our combined resources offered! There were torpedoes, safe for babies, fire-crackers of all sizes, double-headed Dutchmen, Chinese bombs, — to make the day glorious, — and, for the exciting evening (one of the two yearly occasions when I was permitted to stay up beyond bird-time) there were pinwheels that flung out beauty from the top of the hitching post, there were dozens of roman candles with their streams of enveloping fire, and luscious shooting stars, and sky-rockets that rose majestically with a disdainful shriek as they spurned the earth and took a golden road to the sky.

Inter-family feasting at the three homes in turn marked Thanksgiving, Christmas and New Year's Day. It was the laden tree on Christmas Eve that offered the second annual escape from early bed-time rules, in itself enough to key one up to ecstacy, without the added intense joy of mysterious expectation and satisfied possession of the largesse of Santa Claus. A Christmas celebration at Cerritos when I was four stands out distinctly in my memory, — a tall, tall tree, as much as twenty feet high, judged by present standards, stood in the upper chamber whose ceiling, unlifted by an excited imagination, is about eight feet. From that tree came Isabel, my most beloved doll, a small bottle of Hoyt's German Cologne, — how I delighted in perfume, — a small iron stove. The latter was put to a use not contemplated by the patron saint, for I am sure he did not want me to spend the whole of the following morning in duress vile in my bed, because of that stove. This is what happened. After breakfast my almost-twin cousin Harry and I, while our mothers chatted at table, re-visited the scene of the past evening's festivities and wished to bring back some of the joy of it. Drawn curtains gave semi-darkness, candles stolen from the closet under the stairs and placed lighted in the wide window-sills gave a subdued light, and many little stubs of the gay Christmas tapers from the tree made a wonderful illumination under the bed and in the tent made by the turned-back bedclothes.

But it was the fire escaping from the paper-stuffed toy stove which stood on the sheet about the foot of the tree that made us decide to hear the clamoring for admittance of the suspicious mothers, — we had sense enough to summon help when conditions arose with which we were unable to cope. But Harry was cannier than I, for he sent me to open the door where the worried women stood, while he escaped from the far end, going down a ladder from the flat roof of the wing to the tall weeds beyond the huge wood-pile. I was apprehended and punished. He wasn't, not being subject to the same administration of discipline as was I. Then it was that I learned that justice does not always prevail in this world.

This Christmas visit affords my earliest memories of Cerritos, although I know I had been there several times before. It was the long blissful summer when I was seven that packed my mind with vivid pictures and remembrance of joyful activity. Is not seven a peak in childhood, — old enough for self direction, young enough for thrills?

After this visit was over and we departed for nearby Los Angeles to make ourselves a new home my life went on in parallel lines, school days in town, vacation days at the ranches. I should tell of them both at the same time to be truly realistic, but the exigencies of narration make it seem better to write of the two experiences as if they were separate. So first, the ranches.

I have told at length of my birthplace, the San Justo. Although it, as well as the southern ranches, was devoted to sheep raising, there were many differences between them. The houses and gardens at San Justo were of New England type, built and developed according to the early associations of the young men. At the other ranches the homes were of adobe, old ones, handed down from the Mexican period.

The locations and surrounding country also differed greatly. In the north the house stood in a valley between wooded hills, with no wide outlook. The southern houses were each placed on the brow of a mesa, with a view across a characteristic California river which might be a dangerous torrent or a strip of dry sand, according to the season of the year. The eyes could follow across flat lands, treeless, except for a few low-growing willows, to far blue mysterious mountains. It was a very empty land, empty of people and towns, of trees and cultivated fields.

The people on the northern ranch were but two miles from a village, with friends, a post office and a church, and San Francisco, a real city, not far away nor hard to reach. When Aunt Margaret came to Los Cerritos there was not a railroad nor a street car within five hundred miles, and Los Angeles, the small village, was sixteen miles away — by horse power, not gasoline or electricity.

However, distance did not prevent the making of good friends, and the isolation of the frontier life was broken by an occasional visit to San Francisco, one or two trips to distant Maine (Aunt Margaret traveled east on the first through sleeper to go over the new railroad), and by the coming of visitors from neighboring ranches or from away.

On one occasion the ranch welcomed for a week the officers of the flag-ship, *Pensacola,* anchored at San Pedro, including Admiral Thatcher, an old friend of the family, who was in command of the Pacific squadron.

Often there was unexpected company in this land of great distances and few inns. Even after my day wayfarers used occasionally to drop in, so that it was necessary to be prepared to double a meal on short notice. Liebig's Extract of Beef many a time counteracted in soup the weakening effect of quantity-extending water. Locked up in a large tin box a ripening fruit cake awaited an emergency call for dessert, and there was always an unlimited supply of mutton and chickens.

The young people did not have time to be lonely. Uncle Jotham was engaged in building up a large sheep business and Aunt Margaret had her sister for company; she had her children and sufficient help so that she did not suffer any of the hardships that are usually associated with pioneer life. I have observed that if a woman is occupied with a young family, and of a reasonably contened disposition it makes no great difference whether the people outside her home are near or far, few or many; — there are books for spare minutes.

It may be of interest to some to know how we happened to come into Southern California, and something of the history of the ranches, Los Cerritos, "The Little Hills," and Los Alamitos, "The Little Cottonwoods" — beautiful, lilting Spanish names, either one of which would have been preferable to the name chosen by those who bought of the ranch lands and promoted the seaside town of Long Beach. I am glad that we are free of responsibility for the choice of that prosaic name, or for the dubbing of Cerritos Hill, Signal, because of the presence on its top of a tripod used as a marker by surveyors.

When my father sailed up the western coast on the Fourth of July, 1851, the old *S. S. Northerner*, unseaworthy, hugged the coast, nearly wrecking herself by the way, on the rocks at Point Firmin; he, from his place on the deck looked across the mesa to Cerritos Hill, and watched the vaqueros at work with cattle, and like many a later comer, was captivated by the country and determined, if possible, sometime to possess a portion of that land. The time came in 1866, when Flint, Bixby & Co. bought from Don Juan Temple the Rancho Los Cerritos, paying him for it in San Francisco twenty thousand dollars in gold, or about seventy-five cents an acre for the twenty-seven thousand acres, without allowing anything for the fine adobe hacienda with its Italian garden. The reason that this was possible was that the owner was growing old and anxious to settle his affairs so that he might go with his family to spend the remainder of his life in Paris. Moreover, business conditions in Southern California were bad at the time, owing not only to the war depression of the country in general, but also to the disastrous drought during the years '62-'63 and '63-'64, when practically no rain fell. The raising of cattle had been up to this time the chief industry, but with the failure of vegetation thousands of them starved to death. It is told that it became necessary for the citizens of Anaheim, where their fine irrigation system kept their colony green, to use their surrounding willow hedge as a defense and post men to fight off the inrush of the famished cattle. It was the wiping out of this industry that brought about the sale of many of the large holdings of land in Southern California and was the beginning of the development of varied industries and the opening of the land for settlement.

The lands which came into the possession of our family about this time were those of Don Abel Stearns and Don Juan Temple, who were both heavy losers as the result of the drought.

Both of these men came to Los Angeles from Boston before 1830 and were among the first Americans to settle in the pueblo. They married native Californians, became Mexican citizens, and adapted themselves to the life of the community they had chosen for their home; their names occur frequently in all accounts of early Los Angeles affairs. (Mr. Temple married Rafaela Cota.)

They both owned city property. Stearn's home, El Palacio, was on the site of the Baker Block, near the Plaza. In 1859 he built at the rear, facing Los Angeles Street and looking down Aliso the Arcadia Block, named for his wife, Arcadia de Bandini. For this building he used bricks from the first local kiln. In order to complete it he borrowed twenty thousand dollars from Michael Reese on a mortgage on the Rancho Los Alamitos, and because of his large losses of cattle during the great drought he was unable to repay the loan and so lost the ranch.

John Temple's general merchandise store stood where the post office does today. In 1859, the same year that marked the building of the Arcadia Block, he built at a cost of forty thousand dollars and delivered to the city a market house surmounted by a town clock with a bell "fine toned and sonorous." This was the court house of my childhood and its clock ordered our days. It stood where the new Los Angeles City Hall now rises. He, with his brother, F. P. A. Temple, built the fine block that marked the northern junction of Spring and Main Streets and has stood until this day of re-routing of Spring Street. By the way, the cutting out of the diagonal part of this street marks the final disappearance of the last bit of the oldest road in town, that which followed the base of the hills out to the brea pits which were the source of their roofing material. Temple Street was originally a gift of John Temple to the city, and the suggestion that its name be changed to Beverly Boulevard does not meet with the approval of those who know what this man meant to the young city. He might very well become the patron saint of those later men out of the east who come to develop us; for it is due to his public spirit they must trace all the land titles of the city. After we had come under the rule of the United States it seemed advisable to survey Los Angeles but the impecunious city council had no money. Temple provided the necessary three thousand to pay for the Ord Survey upon which all titles are based.

At one time he extended his operations into Mexico where he acquired lands and wealth, part of the latter due to an arrangement with the Mexican government whereby he and his son-in-law performed the functions of a mint, making money for the government on a commission basis.

Those who are interested in seeing pictures of the don and his lady who dreamed and built the Cerritos house and garden may find old portraits in the museum at Exposition Park.

As for the ranches, Cerritos and Alamitos, they were both part of the great grant of land made to Don Manuel Nieto in 1784 by Governor Don Pedro Fages, representing the King of Spain. This grant amounted to about two hundred thousand acres which extended between the San Gabriel and Santa Ana rivers and from the sea back to the first foothills. It was one of three grants made in November of that year to retired soldiers. The others were the San Pedro to Juan José Dominguez and the San Rafael to José Maria Verdugo.

According to Don Antonio Maria Lugo, whose memory went back to 1790, a fourth grant was made before 1800 to Don Juan Pablo Grijalva in the Santa Ana Cañon, but no records of this are found until 1810 when ownership of the Santiago ranch was confirmed to his son-in-law Don José Antonio Yorba, and his grandson, Don Juan Pablo Peralta. Grijalva was a sergeant under Anza on the remarkable enterprise of bringing colonists across desert and mountains from Mexico to California in 1775-76. He brought wife and three little children with him.

From Bernardo Yorba in 1875 my uncle, John W. Bixby, bought a ranch extending from the beautiful cañon of the Santa Ana up over rounded grassy hills. On this his daughter, Mrs. Susanna Bixby Bryant, is now developing as a memorial to him a Botanic Garden of the Native Plants of California, which will preserve our flora, replenish depleted stocks, and make accessible for pleasure and study a collection of our rich store of native plants.

The Yorba properties adjoined those of the Nietos from the foothills to the sea. When Don Manuel Nieto died his lands were divided into four parcels for his heirs. Rancho Santa Gertrudis upon which Downey, Rivera and Santa Fe Springs now stand, went to his son, Antonio Maria Nieto, being later confirmed to his widow, Doña Josefa Cota de Nieto. Los Alamitos, Los Coyotes and Palo Alto were the portion of Don Juan José Nieto, the new head of the family; Los Bolsas was the portion of Doña Catarina Ruiz, and Los Cerritos that of Doña Manuela Nieto de Cota, whose title to it was confirmed in 1834 by Governor José Figueroa on behalf of the Mexican government. In December, 1843, judicial possession was given John Temple, he having paid each of the twelve children of Doña Manuela the sum of two hundred and seventy-five dollars and seventy-five cents. He also paid someone twenty-five dollars for the ranch branding iron and the right to use it. I presume that this went with the ranch and was the familiar triangle with a curly tail that I knew in my childhood. Temple at once proceeded to build his house and lay out his Italian garden.

It was in 1866 that Flint, Bixby & Co. bought the Cerritos. At the time of the purchase my father's younger brother, Jotham Bixby, was made manager and was given the privilege of buying in at any time. In 1869 a half interest was deeded him, and the ranch carried on by him and the older firm under the name of J. Bixby & Co.

When California came under United States rule there ensued much confusion as to land titles and all must be reviewed and passed upon by a specified commission. I have seen a formidable looking transcript of these proceedings in regard to Los Cerritos, copied out in long hand with many a Spencerian flourish, rolled in a red morocco leather cover and tied with blue tape, all of which went to confirm the title of the land to John Temple.

The deed from J. Temple to Flint, Bixby & Co. and the later one of one-half interest from that firm to Jotham Bixby are in the vaults of the Bixby offices in Long Beach.

Because of the possible interest of the many thousand land-holders now in Long Beach and Signal Hill I recapitulate the list of early owners of the land. The first of record is Don Manuel Nieto, 1784; from him it went to his daughter Manuela de Cota and later to her twelve heirs; Don Juan Temple bought it in 1843, and Flint, Bixby & Co. in 1866, selling a half interest to Jotham Bixby in 1869. In 1880 four thousand acres of this were sold to the American Colony under the leadership of W. E. Willmore and from this beginning has gone into the ownership of an untold number. The name at first was Willmore City but was changed to Long Beach about four years later when it was bought by a group of men interested in developing it as a Chautauqua town.

The ranch was held intact for some time after its purchase by my people and used at first almost exclusively for the grazing of sheep, at one time there being as many as thirty thousand upon it. Later cattle were added, not allowed to range at will as in the Mexican days, but confined in large fenced fields or potreros.

Abel Stearns bought the Alamitos three years before John Temple acquired the Cerritos. Nieto had sold it to General Figueroa in 1834 for $500 and he in turn sold it to Stearns in 1840, the consideration being $5500 in hides and tallow, to be laid down in either Mazatlan or San Pedro. Mr. Stearns bought other lands lying between the San Gabriel and Santa Ana rivers until he held about two hundred thousand acres.

There were very neighborly relations between him and the Temples over on the adjoining ranch, — seven miles between houses meant little in those days. A friendly rivalry existed between them as to the relative speed of their horses and a race was an annual affair, the course being from Cerritos Hill to and around a post on the bluff where Alamitos Ave. in Long Beach now reaches the sea, four miles in all. Horse-racing was a favorite sport of the time and many stories have come down to us, among them one of these Temple-Stearns affairs. The stake was a thousand head of cattle and was won by Beserero, Temple's rather ungainly horse. On this occasion there was great rejoicing at Cerritos, celebrations and feasting that lasted all night.

But the lack of rain in '62-'64 ended these halcyon days. Temple sold the Cerritos, dying almost immediately afterward. Stearns lost the Alamitos to Michael Reese, the money lender of San Francisco. My uncle Jotham used to say that this Mr. Reese was famous for his excessive thrift and that he came to his end thereby. It seems that he wished to visit a certain cemetery that charged a five cents admission fee, and that he, in order to save his money, attempted to climb over the wall, but slipped and fell, breaking his neck.

Soon after the drought the whole twenty-nine thousand acres of the Alamitos had been advertised for sale for $153, delinquent taxes, but no buyer appeared. It was acquired in 1866 by Michael Reese, holder of the mortgage.

I have learned from Mr. J. J. Mellus, that in 1866 Gabriel Allen was living in the old adobe on the Alamitos, and had several thousand head of cattle and horses. In 1873 Mr. Mellus' brother-in-law, W. S. Lyon, leased the ranch from Michael Reese for ten years, and Mr. Mellus himself was interested with him in the sheep business. About 1878 these men sub-leased one or two thousand acres to John W. Bixby. He and his wife, Susan Hathaway, and their small son Fred moved in at once.

In 1883 at the termination of the lease of the ranch held by Mr. Lyon the whole property came on the market at a tempting price. The young people to whom this had already been home for five years saw an opportunity that must not be missed, but it was too much to be undertaken alone. The wife had been in California for a number of years and had seen the process by which Jotham with help had been able to change from a small rancher to the prosperous manager and half-owner of the Cerritos and encouraged her husband to make the attempt to do likewise. First he was to see the big Los Angeles banker, I. W. Hellman. He said he would go into this purchase if Jotham Bixby would; the latter said he would if Flint, Bixby & Co. would. They all would and so it came about the Alamitos was secured, Mr. Hellman owning one-third, J. Bixby & Co., another third and young John Bixby in as manager with his third.

This ranch, like the Cerritos, had been cattle range before it became sheep range; unlike the former it has continued to this day as a stock ranch, and although it is many years since there have been sheep it is well known for its cattle, horses, and mules. All the eastern portion of Long Beach, including Bixby Park, that famous center of annual state picnics, came from the Alamitos, and it was John Bixby himself who bought and planted the trees that now shelter the multitudes and afford foci for the gathering of the wandering inhabitants from each and every Iowa county.

Many people now familiar with Southern California have seen the old house surrounded by trees that is on the brow of a hill out on Anaheim Road beyond the Long Beach Municipal Golf Links. That is the old Alamitos Ranch house. When my uncle and aunt first went there to live it was almost a ruin, having fallen during the Reese period from the high estate it had known when it was the summer home of the lovely Arcadia de Bandini de Stearns. The only growing things about it were one small eucalyptus tree and one fair sized pepper tree.

The front room had been used as a calf-pen and the whole house was infested with rats. Uncle John told me that the first night they slept there the baby demanded a drink, and in his passage to the kitchen to secure one he counted sixteen of the rodents. The first improvement they made was to cover all the holes in baseboards and walls with portions of kerosene cans.

It was what grandfather called a "notable housewife" that undertook the rehabilitation of that wreck of a house. Gradually as the young couple got ahead improvements were made, each one to be rejoiced in and enthused about by the interested visiting relatives. I remember when certain doors were cut, when the windows were enlarged, when the first lawn went in, when two fuchsia bushes were brought from Los Angeles, (one of them is still in its place, bravely blossoming), and a rare yellow calla. Aunt Susan took care of the chickens, with the privilege of spending all her returns for books. Great was the occasion when a big stuffed armed chair could be purchased for the young head of the family.

Little by little changes were made in the building itself, that added to both its comfort and its charm. One of the first was the building of a high tank with its cool-house underneath which has served more than forty years for the storing of food; only recently a self-icing refrigerator has come to its aid. To supply this tank with water a busy ram down by the spring, over-hung with willows and decked with water hyacinths, steadily chug-chugged its days and nights away.

A bathroom shortly followed, its installation holding the excited imagination of the children; a little later the house sprouted a wing, containing two bedrooms, "No. 1" and "No. 2," and the moving of dining room and kitchen three times marked the expansion of the home.

The growing habits of the place persist; it is alive. Each time I go back I find some new thing, now a garden, now a modern heating plant skillfully contrived to circumvent the cellarless condition and massive walls, last of all a cactus garden boasting some imported sand to simulate a desert, but crying out for rocks and stones, which are not to be found in adobe soil.

The vision and industry of John Bixby and his wife, continued through the years by their son, Fred Bixby, and his wife, Florence Green, have made from the dilapidated pile of mud bricks one of California's most charming homes. It is a rare thing in this new country to find a house that has been occupied continuously by one family for almost fifty years.

In contrast to this ranch house the one at Cerritos has fallen from its high estate and is now but a shell of its old self. It has long been deserted and has been kept in repair only sufficient to prevent its meeting the fate of neglected adobes, that of melting away under the winter rains.

Little do the many people who daily pass it on their way to Long Beach dream of its former beauty, its gay and busy life.

Don Juan Temple planned and built it about 1844. For it he imported bricks from the East, shipping them around the Horn. They were used in the foundation of the house, for paving two long verandas, for marking off the garden beds, and for lining a sixty-foot well and building a large cistern.

From the northern forests of the state he obtained handhewn redwood which he used for the beams, floors and other interior woodwork, and for the twelve-foot fence about the large garden.

The walls of the house were made from the usual large slabs of sun-dried adobe, made on the spot. They were moulded in frames constructed for making nine or twelve at a time; this frame was laid on a level bit of ground and packed with clay-like mud, into which straw had been tramped by the bare feet of the Indians; when exposure to the sun had caused the shrinking away of the bricks from the wood, the frame was lifted and the slabs left for further drying out.

When I was a child there was a pit below the house, near the river where water could be obtained easily, in which I have watched the mixing of the adobe; I saw the bricks made in small quantities for purposes of repair or the building of a new wall.

The house was built with a two-storied central portion a hundred feet long, with two one-storied wings about one hundred and sixty feet in length, extending toward the river. The ends of these were joined by a high adobe wall in which there was a single gate, its heavy wooden doors being closed at night during its earlier history, but seldom during the later period.

Originally the roofs were flat and roofed in the usual Southern California fashion, first a layer of redwood planks, then a covering of sand or gravel over which was poured hot brea (asphaltum) from the open beds beyond Los Angeles. These were the same brea pits in which in recent years the remarkable discoveries of pre-historic animal bones have been made. In the days when my father and uncles first came to California there were many dangerous wild animals still at large, but fortunately the mastodons and sabre-tooth tigers, hyenas and milder camels were all safely put away in brea storage.

When the summer sun was hot on the roofs the asphalt grew so soft that we could dig it out with sticks and shape it with our fingers. Such depredations undoubtedly contributed to the unsatisfactoriness of the overhead shelter, but even without our intervention the alternate shrinking and expansion of the substance made the roof more or less like a sieve in winter. Uncle Jotham soon tired of dripping rain inside the house, no matter how much he prayed for it outside, so that very soon after he moved into the adobe he added a good old-fashioned Yankee roof to the main portion of the house. The roofs on the wings did not come until after I had learned the joy of the flat ones. Here we used to go at sunset to wait for the homecoming of the fathers, for whose returning buggies we could watch from this vantage ground. We also could see the whole sunset sky, and the lovely pink lights on far, faint Baldy.

The outside of the house, as was the custom with adobes, was kept trim with frequent coats of whitewash; the doors, window frames and slender balusters of the upper veranda railing were a soft green, like the tones on old copper. In the lower story the windows were iron-barred, and in the outer walls of the wing, high up, were funnel-shaped holes through which guns might be shot if any necessity for defense arose.

It may be because of these features that some people have called this an old fort, but it never was one in any other sense than that a man's house is his castle. However the use of guns was more or less free in those old frontier days and an occasion might arise when the man inside might be very glad of a chance to defend himself such as those loop holes afforded.

It was on this ranch that one of the battles at the time of the American conquest of California occurred. It is recorded that the Californians under Carillo here met, one night, Col. Stockton's forces which had landed at San Pedro; the Californians, by driving back and forth in the darkness a large herd of horses, succeeded in giving the impression of a much larger force than they really had. Perhaps they were horses belonging to John Temple and Abel Stearns and to the neighboring Dominguez ranch.

Mr. Benjamin D. Wilson was a semi-prisoner here during the time of this war. He was one of the Americans who had been taken prisoner at the battle at the Chino ranch and was taken with others to Los Angeles. When further hostilities threatened he was sent to the Cerritos under the care of Mr. Temple for safe keeping, by the order of the officer in command of the Californians, who might be technically an enemy of Don Benito, but was before that his friend. This is told in Mr. Wilson's reminiscences.

The approach to the house was through the large gate in the wall that closed the patio. I think the court never was planted to any extent, the garden being on the farther side of the house. It afforded only a few locust trees, one large pink oleander and several hitching posts. There was always much going and coming here, for the ranch business involved the use of saddle horses and carriages. The animals were kept in the barns beyond, but were brought here for all family saddles or carriages. It was a sunny, friendly, busy place, much loved and frequented by the many cats and dogs. I remember also a coon that lived in a far corner for a time and some little coyotes that had been brought in from the range.

In the right wing, next the foreman's room, was the store room, possibly more interesting because it was kept locked and only occasionally did we get access to the dried apples, the chocolate, the brown sugar and the fragrant lead foil that came in the gay boxes of Chinese tea. Many a wise mother-cat entered the fastness through the long window closed only by the iron bars where we could admire but not handle her babies.

One day I discovered a very beautiful heavy white smoke pouring out this window and hurried to find help. Father and the men who came had great difficulty in putting out the fire that had been caused by the drying-out and self-ignition of some stick phosphorous, kept for the preparation of poisoned wheat for use in the war with the squirrels who would have liked to eat up all the wheat we had raised.

Next to the store room was a double-sized room, the usual one being square, the size of the width of the building. Here was a great chimney with a bellows and forge, and on the other side a long bench well-supplied with carpenter's tools. One of our favorite occupations was to hunt up odd pieces of lead pipe, cut them into bits, beat them flat on the anvil and fold over into book-like shapes which we decorated with nail-prick design. I think it speaks something for the tastes of our elders that it was books we made.

Across the court was the kitchen where Ying reigned supreme, and Fan was his prime minister. Later Fan, having passed his apprenticeship, moved on to be head cook at the Alamitos.

When Aunt Margaret had first come to the ranch to live there was no stove in the kitchen, and the first morning she went down

RANCHO LOS CERRITOS IN 1889

RANCHO LOS CERRITOS IN 1931

RANCHO LOS ALAMITOS IN 1887

she found her Indian boy kindling a fire by the friction of a couple of pieces of wood. The baking was done, even after the installation of a range, in a large brick oven out in the rear court, and Saturday afternoon witnessed the perfection of pies, bread, cake. Once I remember feasting on a sand-hill crane, that, too big for the kitchen stove, had been baked in this out-door oven.

I have been asked about the character of the meals and the sources of food supply at the ranches. As was customary at the time there was more served than is usual at present. At breakfast there was always eggs, or meat,—steaks, chops, sausage—potatoes, hot bread, stewed fruit, doughnuts and cheese, and coffee for some of the grown folks. Dinner came at noon and frequently began with soup, followed by a roast, potatoes, two other fresh vegetables, with pickles, olives and preserves. Salads were unknown, but we sometimes had lettuce leaves, dressed with vinegar and sugar. For dessert there were puddings or pies or cake and home-canned fruit, and cheese. It will surprise some of the younger folk to know that mush—either cracked wheat or oatmeal or cornmeal was a supper dish. Sometimes the main article was creamed toast, and there might be hot biscuit, with jelly or honey or jam, and perhaps cold meat, and always again doughnuts and the constant cheese—very new for some tastes and very old for others.

As for the supplies—the meat all came from the ranch. Every day a sheep was killed—occasionally a beef. Uncle John at the Alamitos built a smoke house and cured hams. There were chickens and ducks, tame, or in season, wild.

The staple groceries came from Los Angeles in wholesale quantities—sugar and flour in barrels, navy beans and frijoles and green coffee in sacks, the latter frequently the source of delicious odors from the kitchen oven while roasting; it was daily ground for the breakfast drink, and the sound of the little mill was almost the first indication of stirring life.

At San Justo the vegetables grew in the garden but at the southern ranches they were bought once a week from the loaded express wagon of a Chinese peddler, whose second function was to bring news and company to the faithful ranch cook and his helper. There was always a plentiful supply of vegetables and the quality was of the best. I remember hearing Aunt Susan tell that her man had brought strawberries to the door every week in the year and she had purchased them except on two January occasions when the berries were not quite ripe.

The chief beverage was water, there was some tea and coffee, never wine or other liquor, except the delicious product of the fall cider mill. Whiskey stood on the medicine shelf and I suppose sometimes afforded relief to masculine colds, or insured against possible snake bite—which never occurred.

Oranges, lemons, figs, and grapes grew in the Cerritos garden, and apples and pears in the orchards; peaches, plums, and apricots were bought from peddlers. Much fruit was canned and fresh apple sauce was constant.

The two Chinamen prepared and served three meals a day to the family, three to the regular men, put up noon lunches for those working away from the house, and at the Alamitos three more meals to the nine or ten milkers who could not eat at the same time as the other men. After this digression I return to the listing of the Cerritos rooms.

Next the kitchen came the men's dining room, which contained a long table, covered with oil-cloth and flanked by wooden benches; the constant fragrance of mutton-stew and onions, of frijoles and strong coffee was more attractive to a hungry nose than the odors chastened for the family meals. Harry frequently ate with the men but I couldn't. There are certain disadvantages in being a carefully brought up girl.

Following down the line of rooms in the left wing one came next upon a wood-room which was given over to many tiers of willow wood, a very necessary adjunct to a kitchen when cooking for as many as thirty people must be done with that light wood for fuel.

In the adjoining laundry, lighted only by two doors in the thick walls we could weekly watch, admire, and try to imitate the skillful sprinkling of the clothes in the approved Chinese manner,—a fine spray blown from the mouth. In those days there were no germs!

The last of the series, opening into the court-yard, was the milk room where the rows of shining pans afforded us unstinted supplies of cream both for the interesting barrel-churns and for the table— clotted cream thick enough to spread with a knife upon hot baking powder biscuits, or a steaming baked potato. I am glad I can remember it, for there is no evidence now-a-days that such cream ever was.

A second court off to one side was formed by the row of barns, sheds, the granary, the hen houses, each offering a different chance to play. On one occasion when we had climbed the outside ladder to the high door in the granary, when it was full of wheat, we tried the difficult feat of chasing mice across the top of the huge, soft mass of grain. One small boy who was fast enough to catch a mouse by the tail had the unpleasant experience of having it turn and bury its little teeth in the back of his hand.

. There was a corncrib nearer the barn and I think I must have filled my mouth at some time full of the hard yellow kernels, for otherwise how would I have acquired knowledge of certain sensations to enable me to dream from time to time that my teeth have suddenly all fallen loose into my mouth, very much over-crowding it?

Once across this court I saw a rebellious young colt who objected to being "broken," walk magnificently on his hind legs. It was here that Silverheel, the father of all the colts, and otherwise honored as a trotter who had won races, showed his superior intelligence, when loosed in the barn which was on fire, by dashing out, rolling in the dirt and extinguishing the blaze in his mane. It made so great an impression upon my little cousin Fanny that some time later when her apron caught at a bonfire she promptly followed his example and undoubtedly saved her life by her prompt action.

To enter the house from the court, we stepped up to the brick terrace and through a wide, low door into a short hall that opened directly opposite into the garden. In this hall was a narrow, steep stairway, under which was a fascinating closet where choice bridles and old coats and boots were kept; where there were boxes of mixed nails and bolts and screws and tacks; on the shelf forward could be found some plug tobacco, some small square bunches of California matches, some candles, and a pile of pink bar soap for use at the veranda washstand. I know yet the smell of that closet.

On the right was a door into the parlor, so low that tall Uncle John had to stoop to enter; across the hall was the spare room. All other rooms opened directly on the long outdoor corridor.

The rooms were dimly lighted because the windows were high, rather small, and, on account of the thickness of the adobe wall, deep-set; upstairs there was more light as those walls were but two feet thick, the lower ones being about three. At the Alamitos one of the first things Aunt Susan did was to cut the windows to the floor. This was never done at Cerritos.

The parlor was a small square room with one window to the court and one to the front veranda. The walls were covered with a light flowered paper, and on them hung four steel engravings of the "Voyage of Life," and the familiar picture of Lincoln and his son Tad. A large walnut book-case occupied one side of the room.

Its drawers at the base were filled with blocks and toys for the downstairs delectation of the succession of babies in the home. A Franklin stove in one corner kept us snug and warm when the ocean chill crept inland. The furniture was covered with a maroon leather, a set exactly like the one in the office at San Justo. I associate the reading of many books with one of those comfortable, stuffed chairs, among them *Two Years Before the Mast,* and *Oliver Twist.*

At the table in the center of the room father and Uncle Jotham spent many a long evening over interminable series of cribbage, and my books are punctuated by "fifteen two, fifteen four and a run is eight." Uncle Jotham's convulsive shakings made his amusement visible rather than audible.

One night Nan was desperately ill with the croup and was wrapped up before the fire in this room while one of the older cousins rode in haste to Compton for the doctor. When he returned he tied his horse hurriedly in the stall in the barn, leaving too long a rope, with the result that somehow, during the night, the poor horse became entangled and was strangled to death, a hard reward to him for his successful effort to save the life of a little girl.

Another memory of this room—of a Sunday afternoon. We had all been over to camp-meeting at Gospel Swamp, not that we were much addicted to camp-meeting, but it was the only available service within reach, and of course we had to go to church on Sunday. We sat on wooden benches in the dust under the willows, not an altogether unpleasant change from the usual pew, at least for the children; and Aunt Adelaide, who was camping there for the week, took us to her tent afterward and gave us some watermelon before we drove the few miles back to the ranch. But Uncle Jotham had a more exciting aftermath. He and papa and I were reading in the parlor after dinner when suddenly he gave a tremendous jump and ran upstairs three steps at a time, where we soon heard a great noise of tramping. In a minute or two he came down with a dead lizard almost a foot long spread on his New York *Tri-weekly Tribune.* Evidently it had mounted his bootleg over at camp-meeting and lain dormant for a couple of hours before attempting further explorations. The first jump came when the little feet struck my uncle's knees—harmless, but uncanny.

The usual gathering place for the family was the wide porch where the sun upon the rose vines flecked the floor with shadows. The bricks that paved this open corridor were laid in an herring-bone pattern and we often practised walking with our feet set squarely on them in order to counteract any tendency we might have to pigeon-toedness.

Beside the central door was a space in the wall held sacred and never touched at regular white-washing time. Here was kept a record of the varying heights of the family from year to year so that we could keep track of our growing prowess. Uncle John, at six feet, topped the list for his generation, but was ultimately passed by his son and two nephews.

A Mexican olla well wrapped in wet gunny sacks, and a long handled tin dipper provided convenient drinking facilities, and a tin washbowl, nearby, just outside the dining room door, was a peremptory invitation to clean hands for dinner.

At the other end of the porch, near grandfather's room, was a very long, knotted-twine hammock, in which we rolled ourselves and held tight for a high swing. I had first known this hammock among the trees in the yard at Skowhegan, but it had come to California with grandfather and Aunt Martha. It had belonged to Uncle Philo Hathaway, who, in order to earn money to complete his college course at Amherst, had been cruising a year with Admiral Thatcher as his private secretary. He evidently contracted Panama fever while in Caribbean waters, for on his way home he died and was buried at sea. The loss of this promising young man was a great grief to all who knew him but to his nephews and nieces who had come into this world after he had left it he was a very shadowy figure.

The already long veranda was extended at each end by an arbor, hung with bunches of the small mission grapes, which Harry and I were wont to squeeze in our grimy handkerchiefs over a tin cup for the purpose of making wine.

The garden spread before the porch, at least two acres, shut in from intruders and sheltered from the ocean winds by the high fence. It was laid out in three tiers of four beds, each about fifty feet square, with a wide border about the whole. They were separated by walks, edged with more of the imported brick. Near the house were flowers and shrubs, but further away grapes were planted, and oranges, pomegranates, and figs.

At the end of the rose-shaded path leading from the front door stood a summer house, bowered in the white-blossomed Madeira vine and set in a thick bed of blue-flowered periwinkle, which I never quite dared to invade, lest it harbor a snake. California children were taught never to step where they could not see. Under the seat in this little shelter were kept the mallets and balls for the croquet set. I wonder if others found the mallets attractive crutches; I believe it was as much fun playing lame as it was playing legitimate croquet.

Beyond the summer house was the large brick cistern and the old well. When Mr. Temple first made a garden he provided the necessary water by using a ram in the river. In those days there was much water below the hill for the Los Angeles and San Gabriel united their waters and poured them into the lowland from which there was no good opening into the sea. As a result the bottom lands were wooded and swampy. Then about 1860 floods came that washed open a channel into the ocean, and another great storm caused the river to divide, sending most of its water through what is now known as New River which crosses the Alamitos further east and reaches the sea some ten miles from the old mouth. These changes, together with the increased use of water for vineyards and orchards in Los Angeles, lowered the river level so that Don Temple dug a well, circular, six feet in diameter and sixty feet deep. His Indians drew the water by means of a long well-sweep. Little folk were duly impressed with the danger of the old well, but there wasn't enough fear to prevent an occasional peering into its black depths, and the dropping of a stone that took so long to reach the water below.

When the Americans came the breezes of the sky were summoned to pump the water from a new well outside the fence, and prosaic pipes carried it from the tank under the windmill to all parts of the garden. The cistern thus left unused could be entered by ladders without and within and afforded a diversion from time to time.

All along the fence grew locust trees, whose blossoms are like white wisteria, and at their feet bloomed the pink Castilian roses brought to California by the Spanish padres. Over beyond the croquet ground there was much anise among those roses—anise, the greenest, most feathery growing thing, and withal affording sweet seeds.

In the center of the far side, shading the small gate that led to the wool barn was a very large pepper tree into whose branches we could climb, and near it grew many lilacs. Two of the walks held little bricked islands in which towered old Italian cypresses, whose small, smooth cones my cousin George assured the younger children were bat eggs. That seemed reasonable—there must be some source for the many bats that swooped about at night.

On a certain southeast corner grew the Sweetwater grape, the first to ripen, and directly across the path from it was a curious green rose, one of the rare plants of the place. The blossoms were of the same quality as the leaves, though shaped like petals. They were not pretty, just odd. The pink roses nearby were lovely, and so were the prickly yellow Scotch roses. We loved the rich red of the Gloire de Rosamonde,—isn't that a more attractive name than Ragged Robin, or is it after all too imposing for the friendly, familiar rose? The best one of all was the Chromatella whose great yellow buds hung over the pale green balustrade of the upper balcony, like the Marecial Niel, but larger and more perfect.

In spring, spreading beds of iris were purple with a hundred blossoms and the white ornithogalums, with their little black shoe-buttons delighted us, while, later in the year, there were masses of blue agapanthus and pink amaryllis and scarlet spikes of red-hot-poker. There were no single specimens of flowers, but always enough for us to pick without censure.

The garden did not contain even one palm tree, or a bit of cactus, nor do I remember a eucalyptus tree, a variety belonging to a later importation. There were two large bunches of pampas grass and two old century plants, which we desecrated in the usual child fashion by scratching names and pictures on the gray surface. There were no annuals.

Orange blossoms, honeysuckle, lilac, and lemon verbena, roses, oleander and heliotrope made a heaven of fragrance. For years the bees had stored their treasure in the wall of grandfather's room, which, being a wooden addition to the house, offered a hollow space; the odor of the honey mingled with that of the old leather bindings of his books in the room, and with the flowers outside. The linnets, friendly, and twittering, built about the porch, and the swallows nested under the eaves; the ruby throated and irridescent humming birds darted from flower to flower and built their felt-like nests in the trees, and great lazy, yellow and black butterflies floated by.

And children wandered here and played, or climbed the spreading tree for the heavy figs bursting with their garnered sweetness, or picked crimson kernels from the leathery pomegranates, or lying under the green roof of the low-spread grapevines, told fairy stories while feasting. There seemed no limit to our capacity for eating fruit, and I never knew any one to suffer. One morning at an eating race I won with thirty-two peaches, not large ones, fortunately.

Over by the windmill was a boggy bed of mint, and many a brew of afternoon tea it afforded us,—mint tea in the summer house, with Ying's scalloped cookies, sparkling with sugar crystals, and our mothers for guests.

Note to third edition, 1931. Within the year the old house has awakened to new life. My brother and his wife have lovingly restored this historic place, making it comfortable and beautiful for modern living. They have with skill and care salvaged whatever of the old garden has persisted, and have added new beauty of fruit and flower and tree. The old grape arbor returns, the yellow jasmine, at least fifty years old, lifts its gay blossoms to the roof line, rewarded for its insistent life by a new human attention. Old locust trees have found new life, and a tall olive tree; the cypress tree that bore the "bats' eggs" may do so again for new little Bixbys in days to come. Cerritos is again a home, made so by Llewellyn Bixby, son of Llewellyn Bixby who, with his partners, first purchased it from John Temple.

CHAPTER VIII

The Ranch Story Continued

C O O K I E S were not the only things in which Ying excelled. There were cakes fearfully and wonderfully decorated with frosting curly-cues, and custard pies so good that grandfather always included one with the doughnuts and cheese that little David carried in his lunch basket when he went up to visit his brother on the famous occasion when he slew Goliath with his sling shot.

Grandfather had left his Maine home and now sat on the sunny California porch and charmed his child audience with versions of the Hebrew stories that I judge he did not use in the pulpit of the dignified village church where he had ministered for so many years. But these adaptations existed even then, for I know now that they were not made for us but had served, a generation earlier, to delight our mothers. We learned how Samson's strength returned when, in the temple of the Philistines, the hooting mob threw rotten eggs at him. Grandfather was not unaware of the characteristics of mobs, for he was an avowed abolitionist and advocate of women's rights when they were unpopular causes, although he himself was never favored with eggs. He used to agree with an old Quaker of a nearby town who said, "If a hen wants to crow, thee'd better let her crow."

To return to his stories: there was the legend of David. When the lion attacked his sheep he ran so fast to their rescue that his little coat-tails stuck out straight behind him; when the lion opened his mouth to roar David reached down his throat and caught him by the roots of his tongue and held him, while, with his free hand he pulled his jackknife out of his trouser's pocket, opened it with his teeth, and promptly killed the beast. Then he sat down upon a great white stone and played on his jew's-harp and sang, "Twinkle, twinkle, little star."

I once gave this form of the story in a Sunday School class as an object lesson in earnestness in the pursuit of duty, and when my teacher kindly asked me where it was to be found, assured her that it must be in one of the intervening Bible chapters that had been skipped in our course. Imagine my chagrin as I vainly sought the text. I must have been fourteen years old at the time.

Grandfather not only told us stories, but he opened Sunday to me for secular reading. On my eighth birthday he had given me a copy of Grimm's *Fairy Tales*, and I was revelling in them when a Sunday came. We were settling ourselves on a blanket out on the grass under the big eucalyptus tree at our Los Angeles home for an afternoon with books; mother questioned the wisdom of my reading such a book on that day. She said we would let grandfather decide. I see him yet, looking over the tops of his spectacles at the eager little girl who had interrupted his reading; "I think," he said, "that a book fit to read any day is fit to read on Sunday." I bless the memory of grandfather, willing to give a child his honest judgment, and that that judgment was of a liberal mind.

I remember that about this time there was a governess in the family who was a member of the Universalist denomination and who sometimes pined for her own church; to comfort her, grandfather told her that he would prepare and preach for her a Universalist sermon, which he did the following Sunday. It may be that this small service on the old ranch porch was the first of this faith in Southern California. Grandfather's catholic sympathy for various religious faiths is also illustrated by his friendship with Rabbi Edelman and his frequent attendance upon the services in the old synagogue on Broadway near Second in Los Angeles.

I treasure a small round lacquer box that he bought for me once from a Chinese peddler who had walked the dusty miles from Los Angeles, balancing on a pole over his shoulder the two large covered bamboo baskets, so familiar to the early Californian. The whole family gathered, while on the shady porch were spread the wonders of China.

There were nests of lacquer boxes, with graceful sprays of curious design in a dull gold; bread boats, black outside and vermillion within; Canton china, with pink and green people, flowers and butterflies; teapots in basket cosies, covered cups without handles; chop-sticks and back-scratchers and carved card-cases, all in ivory; feather fans with ivory or sandalwood carved sticks; toys, such as a dozen eggs in decreasing size packed one within another, tiny tortoises with quivering heads and legs in glass-topped green boxes, or perplexing pieces of wood cut into such strange shapes that it took much skill and time to replace the blocks if once disturbed;

there was exquisite embroidery, shawls, or silk handkerchiefs, sometimes there was one of the queer hanging baskets of flowers and fruit fashioned from feathers, silk and tinsel, that so delighted the Chinese themselves but which the housewives rather dreaded receiving as New Year gifts from devoted servants; to top off there was always the strange candy, ginger and lichee nuts. How could so many things come out of those baskets!

If the Chinaman was an essential part of the housekeeping, the Mexican was an integral part of the ranch proper. When Mr. Temple lived at the Cerritos he had great numbers of humble retainers who lived for the most part in huts or *jacals* of tule or willow brush; some of the more favored ones stayed in the wings facing the patio and others occupied the older Cota house that stood near the river.

My cousin, George, who lived at the ranch all his boyhood, once wrote of these people: "The men of these families had been accustomed to work occasionally as vaqueros in the service of the rancho. There was always plenty of meat; and frijoles and chili, with mais del pais were to be raised under crude forms of cultivation at the foot of the hill. On account of the death by starvation of the cattle on the over-stocked ranges the occupation of these people was gone and they soon vanished seeking fields of usefulness elsewhere. . . .

"Among the Temple retainers, however, was one strong and stalwart character, the most perfect horseman and acknowledged leader of the vaqueros, Juan Cañedo. He was manifestly attached to the land by strong ties of sentiment, and set up the claim that Mr. Temple had sold him with the ranch to Mr. Bixby, with whom he intended to stay. . . . This man was expert in the use of the reata—the left hand as well as the right—and was easily superior to any of those now exhibiting in the wild west shows. For those days this sort of thing was the life of the people, not their pastime, and this was a picked man among them."

George knew and loved Old Juan as long as he lived, provided for his old age, stayed with him when he died, and for many years paid monthly the widow's grocery bill.

When the little boy was four his father had a saddle made especially for him and Juan delighted to show him how to ride, to make a horseman of him; he also served as a teacher of Spanish. Juan never condescended to speak English, although he understood it, so my conversations with him were one sided, for I regret to say that my knowledge of Spanish was very meager.

He looked like a bronze statue, brown face, brown clothes, brown horse and infinite repose. Many a time have I seen him ride out of the courtyard gate followed by the hounds, Duke, Queen, Timerosa, and others of forgotten name, to hunt coyotes, the constant menace to the sheep.

There were many other interesting men who worked at the ranches. There was always a José; I remember a romantic looking Romulo, and Miguel, who is now spending his last days a tenant of the old house. Over at Alamitos there was a jolly, fat vaquero with a heavy black beard and twinkling eyes, who was known as "Deefy" —I spell phonetically—because scarlet fever at twelve had stolen his hearing. He remembered enough of language to speak, but did so in the most uncanny, guttural and squeaking sounds. He was a friendly soul and never so appalling as dignified Old Juan.

Then there were all sorts of other nationalities represented in one way or another; Parlin, a Maine man, always predicting disaster, and speaking only in a whisper; Roy, the Englishman, John "Portugee," Henry and Charlie, young Americans getting a start, and the merry Irish John O'Connor who always had time for a joke with the children, and whose departure was mourned when he left the Cerritos to open a saloon on Commercial Street in Los Angeles.

Just a few years ago at Uncle Jotham's funeral in Long Beach I was touched to see a whole pewful of these men who had worked for him in the old days at the ranch, even John O'Connor among them.

I recall Sunday evenings at the Alamitos when Uncle John got out his fiddle, and men who had other instruments came into the parlor and we had a concert that included *Arkansaw Traveler*, *Money Musk* and *Turkey in the Straw*. There had been a piano in the parlor at the San Justo, but neither Cerritos nor Alamitos boasted piano or organ.

To this day the employees on the Alamitos come to the home for merry-making at least once a year when the hostess provides a Christmas party with a tree and candy and a present for everyone connected with the ranch, from the great-grandmother of the family down to the last little Mexican or Japanese that lives within its borders.

Although sheep were the earliest interest gradually cattle were added. Once upon a time in California there had been no fences and cattle wandered freely, being sorted and claimed by their owners once a year at the great rodeos. Now they were confined within the limits of a ranch by bordering fences. We had cattle on both the Alamitos and the Cerritos but the greater range was on the Palos Verdes. Those were exciting mornings when, at dawn, the men and boys started off for the round-up on the hills beyond Wilmington, Uncle Jotham and father in the single buggy with two strong horses that would take them up and down ravines and over the hills where no roads were. I have been told that sometimes they would ride along a hillside where the slant was so steep that in order to prevent the carriage from tipping over men on horse-back would fasten their reatas to the upper side and ride above them. The rodeo days were great days for the boys. I couldn't go, I was a girl and must be a lady,—whether I was one or not.

But fashions change, and the Alamitos girls today have always been horsewomen with their father, and can handle cattle better than most men; and then they can lay aside their ranch togs and don a cap and gown and hold their own in a college, or in filmy dress and silver shoes, grace a city dance,—competent and attractive daughters of California.

Aunt Susan, grandmother to these girls, was most hospitable, especially to children, and Uncle John, with his jokes and merry pranks, a delight to them. I shall always hear the sound of his voice as he came in the back door of the hall, danced a sort of clog and called some greeting to his little wife. He always wore at the ranch boots with high heels,—cowboy boots.

Often there would be gathered at the Alamitos, in addition to the children who belonged, half a dozen cousins with their friends, and the small Hellmans, whose father was a part owner in the ranch. The house was elastic, and if there were not beds enough there were mattresses and blankets to make warm places on the floor. The privilege of sleeping in the impromptu bed was a much coveted one.

A favorite resort was the great barn, a still familiar sight to passers-by on the Anaheim Road. It was made from an old government warehouse taken down, hauled over from Wilmington and rebuilt at the ranch, forty-odd years ago. It afforded magnificent leaps from platform to hay or long slides on the slippery mows. Up among the rafters were grain bins, whose approach over narrow planks added a spice of danger—a mis-step would have meant a thirty-foot fall, but we never made mis-steps. In the central cupola Fred and Nan kept house, while the babies were parked in the bins.

"Old Sorrel," a friendly mare, lived down in the pasture beyond the wool-barn, and might be ridden for the catching. She seemed to like to carry a backful of small people, extending from her mane to her tail. Fred had a real horse, "Spot," for riding but "Sorrel" was the playmate. Harry had one of those favored horses of old California, cream-colored with silvery trimmings, and he called him by the general name of his kind, "Palomino."

There were fish to be caught in New River below Alamitos, cat-fish and carp that could be taken home and eaten. One day Fred and I, wandering about, came upon some that had been speared and left by poachers. We were indignant, but could do nothing to the men we saw drive away. However, we could prevent the waste of good fish, so we took them to the house, neglecting to tell the cook that we had not just killed them ourselves. They could not have been too dead, for no one suffered for eating them.

Kittens and puppies abounded and new chickens, pigs, and calves or colts provided constant interest. Once when two insig-nificant little dogs were assisted out of the world little Sue took comfort in thinking they would look very cute in Heaven tagging around after God every time He went for a walk.

The son of the house staged one spring a new entertainment. His father took great pride in his first litter of twelve thorough-bred Berkshires, and every day each member of the family in-spected the new pigs. One day the son of the chief dairyman dared the boy to kill them, which dare he immediately accepted, doing the execution with a pitchfork. Then followed a thrashing, weep-ing and wailing and gnashing of teeth and no more slaughterings!

I was not involved in this affair, but I cannot claim blood-guilt-lessness. I recall with a shudder my participation in the stabbing of fat frogs in a shallow pool; even then it sent shivers up and down my spine, but I could do almost anything the boys could. I did draw the line at knocking down swallows' nests and feeding the baby birds to the cats, although Harry maintained that this was necessary to prevent the introduction of bed-bugs from the nests into the house. A year or two later the boy went out with a new gun that had been given him, but came back telling me that he could not shoot turtle doves who sat in so friendly a fashion to-gether on the fence rail and made mournful sounds, neither could he shoot rabbits, for they looked at him. He was a sensitive boy and the earlier killings belonged to our primitive stage of develop-ment.

In those days I frequently watched, in spite of mother's wish that I should not, the daily butchering of a sheep, not so much the actual slaying, but the skinning and the removal of the slippery, interesting insides; a daily course in anatomy. And blown-up bladders made wonderful playthings.

One of the most interesting features of the Alamitos was the cheese-making that was done on a large scale, two hundred cows being milked for the purpose night and morning. To improve the milk for this Uncle John imported some of the first registered Holsteins into Southern California. There was great excitement among us children, and undoubtedly a fair degree of it among the grown-ups, when a carload of fine animals arrived from New York, prominent among them being several members of the Holstein family of Aaggie, a magnificent bay stallion, and about a dozen Shetland ponies. For a number of years Mrs. Bixby's span of these harnessed to a tiny buggy were a familiar sight about Long Beach.

She was a skillful driver and I shall never forget a night ride I had with her when I was a little girl. I was going home with her from Los Angeles for a few days at the ranch. We took the train at the Commercial Street station at about five o'clock, and when we reached Wilmington at six it was already dark. We went to the livery stable where the teams had been left for the day, and then set out for the ranch, Uncle John in his gig with Fred, the small boy, tucked in under the seat. In the wide, single-seated buggy drawn by two lively horses, Aunt Susan drove, with me between her and the nurse, who held the baby girl. The night was so dark and the fog so thick that we could not see the horses' heads, much less the road. We followed close to my uncle, who called back every few minutes, and found the way across the bridge and started along Anaheim Road, not a street lined with houses as it now is, but just a track across the bare mesa. It was before the day of Long Beach.

Slowly, slowly, we went along, almost feeling our way, blind-folded by the mist. There was not a light or a sound, and soon we lost Uncle John, but Aunt Susan did not fail in courage and told us she was going to give the horses their head and trust them to take us home. By and by, after two hours they came to a stop and we found we were on the brow of the hill above the wool barn, just a few steps from the house. It was relief enough for me to have come home; what must it have been to the woman driving!

One other foggy drive I took many years later. I was fifteen and had been for several days at the Alamitos, among other things making diagrams of spots of some Holstein calves on the blanks of application for registration, that being a privilege reserved for me, the wielder of the pencil among us. In order to be back in school Monday morning, I had to be taken over to Long Beach to meet the first Los Angeles train. How many times have I eaten lamp-lit breakfasts in the old ranch dining room and started off in the sweet fresh morning, to watch the dawn and hear the larks sing as we drove!

This foggy morning Uncle John was driving and as it was April there was a pearly light over everything. Every hair of his beard and eyebrows was strung with tiny drops of water; we had a most happy hour, drawn by Thunderbolt and Lightfoot. The next day came word of sudden sickness. In ten days my merry young uncle was dead. It did not seem possible. It was my first realization of death. And childhood ended! When my mother had gone I was ten, and while it seemed strange, it did not stand out from all the strangeness of the world as did this later coming face to face with the mystery. In the case of my mother I missed her more as years went by than I did at the time of the actual separation.

Aunt Martha was distressed when after mother's death she came to us, to find how often we children played that our dolls had died. We held a funeral service and buried them under the sofa in the parlor after a solemn procession through the long hall. We wore towels over our heads for mourning veils, copied not from any used in our family, but from those of two tall, dark sisters who sat in front of us in church, whose crepe-covered dresses and veils that reached the floor were a source of unfailing wonder.

As I look back it does not seem to me that the playing of funerals involved any disrespect or lack of love for our mother, but was, rather, a transference into our daily activities of a strange experience that had come to us.

We had another play that was connected with a death, but at the time I did not recognize the relationship. Just before we came south for the long visit, Harry's five-year-old sister Margaret had died of diphtheria and was buried in the ranch garden. Soon after our arrival a mason came and set up a gravestone for her. Beside her grave were those of an older sister, and of a little unnamed baby. The ranch had been robbed of its children and the heart of the young mother sorrowed. Harry had been devoted to Maggie and was disconsolate without her, so that I must have been a most wel-

SHEEP DIPPING AT RANCHO LOS CERRITOS IN 1872

Jotham Bixby in center

come visitor for the lonely small boy. Taking our cue from the
mason we spent many hours in the making of mud tombstones for
our bird and animal burial plot over near the graves of the children.
I modelled them and he polished them and put on the inscriptions.

We wandered about day after day, in the cool summer sunshine,
—so near the ocean that oppressive heat was rare. As soon as breakfast was over, away we went. I was clad in a daily clean blue-and-
white checked gingham apron, Harry, although but seven, in long
trousers, "like the men." We romped in barn or garden, visited
the corrals or gathered the eggs; we played in the old stage left
in the weeds outside the fence, or worked with the tools in the
blacksmith shop. When the long tin horn sounded at noon the call
for the men's dinner we returned to the house to be scrubbed. I
was put into a white apron for mealtime, but back into my regi-
mentals as soon as it was over. A second whitening occurred for
supper and lasted until bedtime.

Sometimes we went down to the orchard, where all summer long
we could pick ripe apples and pears; and occasionally, as a rare
treat, we were allowed to go barefoot and play in the river, reduced to its summer safe level. One day, after having built elaborate sand houses and laid out rival gardens, planted with bits of
every shrub and water weed we could find, we went to a place deep
enough for us to sit down in water up to our necks, where, grinning
over the top of the water, we enjoyed an impromptu bath. We
hung our clothes on a willow until they were dry and then wondered what uncanny power made our mothers know that we had
been wet.

A half mile or so beyond this ford lived Uncle Marcellus and
Aunt Adelaide, and their boys, Edward and Herbert, who used to
come over to help at shearing time. Just inside their front door
they had a barometer shaped like a little house where a woman
came out and stood most of the time, but if it were going to rain
the gallant husband sent her inside and stood guard himself.

The largest and loveliest hyacinths I have ever known grew for
this aunt, and she had tame fish in her pond that would come and
eat breadcrumbs which we gave them. Aunt Adelaide was a very
short woman with the shiniest, smooth, dark hair that never turned
gray. It went in big waves down the side of her face. Once she
showed mother a number of large new books and told her about a
way to study at home and learn just as if you were going to college, and a long time afterwards she showed us a big piece of paper

that she said was a Chautauqua diploma and meant that she had studied all those books.

Every time we went over to the station on the railroad, or came back, or went to Compton to church or camp meeting, or came back, we always saw the old house that had been the first ranch house, belonging to the Cotas, but which had now only pigeons, many, many shining lovely pigeons and one great mysterious white owl living in it,—and so many fleas that we called it the "Flea House" and knew better than ever to go into it.

But we were not afraid to go into the deserted coyote hole that we found in a bank down on the side of the hill below the house. Luckily we did not find a rattlesnake sharing it with us.

The sum of child happiness cannot be told. How good it is to wander in the sun, smelling wild celery, or the cottonwood leaves, nibbling yellow, pungent mustard blossoms while pushing through the tangle; how good to feel a pulled tule give as the crisp, white end comes up from the mud and water, or to bury one's face in the flowing sulphur well for a queer tasting drink, or to cut unnumbered jack-o-lanterns while sitting high on a great pile of pumpkins of every pretty shape and color, and singing in the salty air; how good to wander in the sun, to be young and tireless, to have cousins and ranches!

CHAPTER IX

Flocks and Herds

S H E E P were the main interest of the ranches, in fact were the prime reason for them. I do not know how many there were all told, but on the Cerritos alone there were often as many as thirty thousand head, and upwards of two hundred thousand pounds of wool were marketed annually in San Francisco. At first the wool was shipped from Newport Landing, but in my day it went from San Pedro.

There was little demand for mutton in the south, so from time to time, in order to dispose of aged surplus stock a band of several thousand sheep would be driven overland to San Francisco. The start would be made in the spring when the grass was green on the hills, so that as the stock moved slowly on they found good feed and reached the city happy and fat,—to meet their doom.

There had been some sheep in California ever since the first ones had been brought in by the padres. But the wool was coarse and of a low grade. Although at the height of the prosperity of the missions there had been large flocks the numbers dwindled after the disestablishment, and were still further lowered by the sale of sheep to the miners in '49 for mutton. This left the field open for such enterprises as that of our people, the Hollisters and others. A good grade of sheep from the middle west, sturdy enough to survive crossing the plains was bettered by the introduction of thoroughbred Vermont and New York merino rams. The sheep prospered under favorable climatic conditions. Coyotes were the chief hazard and the effort to outwit them must have offered the only spice in life to the sheep herder and his dogs.

We shared in the improvement of the quality of California wool. I remember at the San Justo a majestic ram with wool that hung to the ground and great curling horns who lived with a few favored wives in the fine-sheep barn up the hill behind the house. The little girl was warned not to be friendly with him since he was neither kind nor gentle. At the Cerritos the thoroughbreds had their comfortable housing just where the Virginia Country Club has built its charming house.

It was only the few aristocrats, however, that had well-built, sheltering homes. The common herd lived out on the range in bands of about two thousand, under the care of a sheep herder and several dogs. These men lived lonely lives, usually seeing no one between the weekly visits of the wagon with supplies from the ranch. Many of the men were Basques. Often there was some mystery about those who took this work,—a life with the sheep was far away from curious observation, and served very well for a living grave. Once I overheard talk of a herder who had been found dead in his little cabin. He had hanged himself. And no one knew what tragedy in his life lay behind the fatal despondency!

One of the men who had been a cabinet maker made me a set of tiny furniture out of cigar boxes,—a cradle, table, bureau, bookcase and three chairs, all delicately fashioned and showing him to be a skilled craftsman. I suppose this man so cut off from normal human relationships enjoyed the occasional visits of the little girl who rode about the ranch with her father.

Every week a man from the ranch made the rounds of the sheep camps, carrying mail, tobacco, and food,—brown sugar, coffee, flour, bacon, beans, potatoes, dried apples. On the morning when this was to happen I have watched the flickering light of the lantern travel back and forth over the ceiling of the room where I was supposed to be asleep, as the finishing touches were put on the load, and the horses were brought and hitched to the wagon before daylight, so that the long rounds could be made before night.

Twice a year, spring and fall, the sheep came up to be sheared, dipped and counted. Father usually attended to the count himself as he could do it without confusion. He would stand by a narrow passage between two corrals, and as the sheep went crowding through he would keep tally by cutting notches in a willow stick.

During shearing time we heard new noises out in the dark at night, after we were put to bed, the candle blown out, and the door to the upper porch opened. Always there were crickets and owls and howling coyotes, and overhead the scurrying footsteps of some mouse on its mysterious business, or the soft dab of an errant bat on the window, but now was added the unceasing bleat of thousands of sheep in a strange place, and separated, ewe from lamb, lamb from ewe.

Shearing began on Monday morning, and on Sunday the shearers would come in, a gay band of Mexicans on their prancing horses, decked with wonderful, silver-trimmed bridles made of rawhide or braided horsehair, and saddles with high horns, sweeping stirrups, and wide expanse of beautiful tooled leather. The men themselves were dressed in black broadcloth, ruffled white shirts, high-heeled boots, and high-crowned, wide sombreros which were trimmed with silver-braided bands, and held securely in place by a cord under the nose. They would come in, fifty or sixty strong, stake out their caballos, put away their finery, and appear in brown overalls, red bandanas on their heads, and live and work at the ranch for more than a month, so many were the sheep to be sheared. They brought their own blankets and camped out. Their meals were prepared in a cook wagon.

Once at the Alamitos, a number of men had sleeping places in the hay in the old adobe barn, each holding his chosen bed most jealously from invasion. Half a dozen of us children, starting after breakfast on the day's adventure, after taking slices from the raw ham stolen from the smoke-house and secreted in the hay, spied some clothes carefully hung on the wall above the mow, and the idea of stuffing the clothes into the semblance of a man was no sooner born that it was adopted. Our whole joy was in doing a life-like piece of work. Fan gave us a paper bag for the head, which we filled and covered with the hat. Little we knew how seriously a hot-tempered Mexican might object to being fooled. In the evening when the men came into the barn the owner of the particular hole in which our dummy was sleeping was furious at finding his place occupied. He ordered the stranger out. No move. He swore violently. Still no move. He kicked. And as he saw the man come apart and spill out hay instead of blood, his rage knew no bounds, his knife came out, and it was only by good luck that we children were not the cause of a murder that night. Uncle John made rather vigorous remarks to us about interfering with the workmen.

There were wool-barns at all three of the ranches that I knew, but I officiated at shearing most often at the Cerritos. Here the barn was out beyond the garden, facing away from the house, and toward a series of corrals of varying sizes. The front of it was like a covered veranda, with wide cracks in the floor. Opening from this were two small pens into which a hundred sheep might be turned. The shearer would go out among these sheep, feel critically the wool on several, choose his victim and drag it backward, holding by one leg while it hopped on the remaining three to his regular position. Throwing it down, he would hold it with his knees, tip its head up, and begin to clip, clip, until soon its fleece would be lying on the floor, the animal would be dismissed with a slap, and the wool gathered up and placed on the counter that ran the length of the shearing floor. Here the grown boys of the family tied each fleece into a round ball and tossed it into a long sack that hung in a nearby frame, where a man tramped it down tight. When the Mexican delivered his wool at the counter he was given a copper check marked J. B., the size and value of a nickel, which he presented Saturday afternoon for redemption. It is a fact that frequently the most rapid workmen did not get the most on pay day, simply because they were less skillful or lucky as gamblers than as shearers.

I remember going one evening into the garden and peering through a knot-hole at a most picturesque group of men squatting about a single candle on the wool-barn floor, playing with odd looking cards, not like the ones in the house. The pile of checks was very much in evidence.

George told me that it was his father's custom for many years to carry the money for the ranch payroll from Los Angeles to Cerritos in a small valise under the seat of his buggy, sometimes having several thousand dollars with him. This habit of his must have been known, but he was never molested. George maintained that there was a code of honor among the prevalent bandits to respect the old citizens so far as possible.

I had beautiful days during shearing. Sometimes I was entrusted with the tin cup of copper checks and allowed to deal them out in return for the fleeces delivered. I spent much time up on this same counter braiding the long, hanging bunches of twine that was used for tying up the fleeces into balls. I worked until I became expert in braiding any number of strands, either flat or round. A few times I was let climb up the frame and down into the suffocating depths of the hanging sacks, to help tramp the wool, but that was not a coveted privilege, — it was too hot and smelly. I loved to watch the full sack lowered and sewed up and then to hold the brass stencils while the name of the firm and the serial number was painted on it before it was put aside to wait for the next load going to Wilmington. Never was there a better place for running and tumbling than the row of long, tight wool sacks in the dark corner of the barn.

Many a check was slipped into our hands, that would promptly change into a watermelon, fat and green, or long and striped, for during the September shearing there was always, just outside the door, a big "Studebaker" (not an auto in those days) full of melons, sold always, no matter what the size, for a nickel apiece. It has ruined me permanently as a shopper for watermelons; nothing makes me feel more abused by the H. C. L. than to try to separate a grocer and his melon.

I seem to have gotten far away from my subject, but, really I am only standing in the brown mallows outside the open end of the wool-barn, watching the six-horse-team start for Wilmington with its load of precious wool that is to be shipped by steamer to "The City," San Francisco, the one and only of those days.

As soon as the shearing was well under way the dipping began. This was managed by the members of the family and the regular men on the ranch. In the corral east of the barn was the brick fireplace with the big tank on top where the "dip" was brewed, scalding tobacco soup, seasoned with sulphur, and I do not know what else. This mess was served hot in a long, narrow, sunken tub, with a vertical end near the cauldron, and a sloping, cleated floor at the other. Into this steaming bath each sheep was thrown; it must swim fifteen or twenty feet to safety, and during the passage its head was pushed beneath the surface. How glad it must have been when its feet struck bottom at the far end, and it could scramble out to safety. How it shook itself, and what a taste it must have had in its mouth! I am afraid Madam Sheep cherished hard feelings against her universe. She did not know that her over-ruling providence was saving her from the miseries of a bad skin disease.

Now the sheep are all gone, and the shearers and dippers are gone too. The pastoral life gave way to the agricultural, and that in turn to the town and city. There is Long Beach. Once it was a cattle range, then sheep pasture, then, when I first knew it, a barley field with one small house and shed standing about where Pine and First Streets cross. And the beach was our own private, wonderful beach; we children felt that our world was reeling when it was sold. Nobody knows what a wide, smooth, long beach it was. It was covered near the bluffs with lilac and yellow sand verbenas, with ice plant and mesembryanthemum and further out with shells and piles of kelp and a broad band of tiny clams; there were gulls and many little shore birds, and never a footprint except the few we made, only to be washed away by the next tide. Two or three times a summer we would go over from the ranch for a day, and beautiful days we had, racing on the sand, or going into the breakers with father or Uncle Jotham who are now thought of only as old men, venerable fathers of the city. Ying would put us up a most generous lunch, but the thing that was most characteristic and which is remembered best is the meat broiled over the little driftwood fire. Father always was cook of the mutton chops that were strung on a sharpened willow stick, and I shall never forget the most delicious meat ever given me, smoky chops, gritty with the sand blown over them by the constant sea breeze. I wonder if the chef of the fashionable Hotel Virginia, which occupies the site of our outdoors kitchen, ever served the guests so good a meal as we had on the sand of the beautiful, empty beach.

CHAPTER X

El Pueblo de Nuestra Señora La Reina de Los Angeles

LOS ANGELES was about ninety years old and I about one when we first met, neither of us, I am afraid, taking much notice of the other. For over twenty years San Francisco had been a city, a most interesting and alive city, making so much stir in the world that people forgot that Los Angeles was the older pueblo; that her birth had been ordained by the governor and attended with formal rites of the church and salutes from the military way back in 1781, when the famous revolution on the east coast was just drawing to a successful close. It is true that in 1776 the Presidio and Mission of San Francisco had been established following the arrival of the group of colonists brought from Mexico over deserts and mountains to California by Juan de Anza, a most remarkable feat, but the first house in Yerba Buena, the forerunner of the great city, was not built until 1836. Before the stirring days of '49, San Francisco was insignificant on sand hills. Then her rise was sudden and glorious and the Queen of the Angels was humble. But she was angelic only in name. She was a typical frontier town with primitive, flat-roofed dwellings of sun-dried bricks, much like those built in ancient Assyria or Palestine. Saloons and gambling houses were out of proportion in number, and there were murders every day. The present crime wave is nothing in comparison.

My father first saw Los Angeles in January, 1854, when he was camped with his sheep on the Rancho San Pasqual; his arrival was a few months later than that of Mr. Harris Newmark, who, in his book *Sixty Years in Southern California*, so vividly describes the village as he found it.

By the time I knew it there had been a great change. There were some sidewalks, water was piped to the houses, gas had been introduced; several public school buildings had been built; there were three newspapers, *The Star*, *The Express*, and *The Herald*. The public library had been founded, — it occupied rooms in the Downey Block where the Federal Building now stands, and Mary

Foy, one of Los Angeles' distinguished women, had begun her public service as a young girl in attendance. Compared with what it had been twenty years before, Los Angeles was a modern, civilized city; compared with what it is now, it was a little frontier town. At school I once learned its population to be 11,311.

We lived first on Temple Street, near Charity. Once Los Angeles boasted Faith and Hope Streets as well, but only Hope remains, for Faith has turned to Flower, and Charity masquerades as Grand.

Next door to us lived a Jewish family whose girls sat on the front porch and amazed me by crocheting on Sunday. I had not known that any Jews existed outside the Bible. Perhaps this family was the nucleus for the present large colony of Hebrews that now fills the neighborhood.

Temple Street was new and open for only a few blocks. Bunker Hill Avenue was the end of the settlement, a row of scattered houses along the ridge fringing the sky. Beyond that we looked over empty, grassy hills to the mountains. Going down the first hillside and over towards Beaudry's reservoir for a picnic, I once found maidenhair ferns under some brush, and was frightened by what sounded like a rattlesnake — probably only a cicada. Court Street disappeared in a hollow at Hope, where a pond was made interesting by a large flock of white ducks.

Across the street from us on top of a hill that is now gone, at the head of a long flight of wide steps, stood The Horticultural Pavilion, destroyed a few years later by fire. It was replaced by Hazard's Pavilion, an equally barn-like, wooden building on the site of the present Philharmonic Auditorium. The first Pavilion held county fairs, conventions, and operas. It was in this place that I once had a great disappointment, for when I was hearing *Pinafore* a child ahead of me suddenly coughed and whooped, and I was removed with haste just at the most entrancing moment. The opera had been put on in London first in the spring of '78. It had reached Los Angeles by '79, and we revelled in its wit and melody with the rest of the world.

It must have been somewhat later than this that the city took such pride in the singing of one of its own girls, Mamie Perry (Mrs. Modini-Wood) who was educated abroad and made her debut in Italy. Another name that will recall many a concert and social event to old timers is that of Madame Marra.

In this building I once saw a strange instrument, a box into which one could speak and be heard half a mile away at a similar contraption — a very meek and lowly promise of our present telephone system.

At this fair, where there were exhibited fruits, jellies and cakes, quilts and long strings of buttons, when the mania for collecting them was at its height, I remember that some ladies, interested in the new Orphans' Home, served New England dinners, in a room decked as an old fashioned kitchen with spinning wheels and strings of corn and drying apples. Among them were my mother and Mrs. Dan Stevens, two slender, dark-haired young women, wearing colonial costume and high combs — my mother, who so soon after left this world, and Mrs. Stevens, still among us, loved and honored for her many good works.

Mrs. Stevens tells me that this was at the time of the visit of President and Mrs. Hayes and a party of government officials, the first president of the United States to come to California. All Los Angeles turned out to welcome them, although there was enough bitter partisan feeling left to cause some neighbors of ours to walk past him in line while refusing to shake the hand of the man who they believed usurped Tilden's rightful place.

The celebration began with speaking from a grandstand built in front of the Baker Block, followed by a reception given to Mrs. Hayes and the ladies of the party in the parlors of the fashionable St. Elmo Hotel, still standing but now fallen to low estate.

After this the presidential party went to the county fair at the pavilion where there was more speaking, a public reception and a formal dinner. Dr. David Barrows contributes as his memory of this great occasion — the memory of a small boy who had been brought down from the Ojai Valley — his amazement to observe that Secretary Sherman kept his cigar in his mouth while making his address. It was during this speech that a little boy came forward bringing a great bouquet, the gift of the local florist, but suffered so from stage fright that he refused to mount the platform and my small sister, standing near, was substituted. She marched serenely across the stage, delivered the flowers to Mrs. Hayes, was kissed by her, then by the speaker, and final glory, by the President himself. I am sure it was the most lime-lighty moment of Nan's modest life.

This bouquet was not the only gift we afforded our distinguished visitor. The other was a cup and saucer, fearfully and wonderfully made of sectors of red, white and blue cambric, stitched round and round until it was stiff, by a little hole-in-the-wall sewing-machine agent.

After inspecting our fruits, vegetables, cookery, button strings and other fancy work the party was entertained at dinner by the leading women of Los Angeles in the improvised New England kitchen at the fair. The city council granted them the privilege and appropriated toward expense the generous sum of twenty-five dollars, all the council could afford toward banqueting the most distinguished party that had yet visited the City of the Queen of the Angels, so said Mayor Toberman. But every grower of fine turkeys or prize fruit or vegetables and every notable maker of preserves brought in offerings in kind so that in spite of the council's thrift a most generous feast was spread before our guests.

Speaking of politics recalls the wonderful torchlight processions of a later period when I, with my cousins, shouting little Republicans, perched on the fence at their residence on the corner of Second and Broadway and delightedly recognized our fathers under the swinging, smoky lights.

I happened to be in Maine during the Blaine-Cleveland campaign and once rode upon a train to which Mr. Blaine's special car was attached. It interested me to see that when he got out at one station for a hasty cup of coffee at a lunch counter, he poured the hot liquid into his saucer to drink. Was that doing politics, being one of the people, or was it simply that the mouth of a presidential candidate is as susceptible to heat as that of an ordinary mortal? I was much edified, as I was not accustomed to saucer-drinking. When the train reached Boston towards midnight, it was met by a most gorgeous torchlight parade and a blare of music.

When Garfield died, Los Angeles had a memorial service and a long daylight procession headed by a "Catafalque," (a large float, gruesomely black), on which one of my schoolmates, Laura Chauvin, rode to represent a mourning angel. Later the black broadcloth draperies of the float were used to make souvenirs and sold for some deserving cause. We purchased a pin-ball the size of a dollar, decorated with a green and white embroidered thistle, — a curious memento of a murdered president.

Mrs. Gibson tells me of another disposition of the black symbols of public mourning. At the time of the assassination of James King of William feeling in San Francisco ran high. The stores were swept clean of every kind of black cloth for the draping of houses as well as public buildings, their home like others being generously hung. The day of mourning past, thrift would not allow the waste of such good material. And so for what seemed a long long time in the life of the little girl she had no clothes but black.

But I have been lured by memories of processions as is a small boy by martial music, away from my ordered account of where I have lived in Los Angeles. The second year we moved to the Shepherd house, (so-called because of its owner), where presently my brother, Llewellyn Bixby, junior, in direct answer to my prayers, came through the ceiling of the front bedroom straight into the apron of Mrs. Maitland, — a two-day late birthday present for me. So I was told. My sceptical faculty was dormant.

This house still stands at the top of the precipice made by the cutting of First Street between Hill and Olive Streets.

The lot in front was very steep, with zig-zag paths and terraces, in one of which was a grove of banana trees, where fruit formed, but, owing to insufficient heat, never ripened well. Do you know the cool freshness of the furled, new, pale green leaves? Or how delightful it is to help the wind shred the old ones into fringe? One by one the red and gray covers for the circled blossoms drop, and make fetching little leather caps for playing children.

In those days the hill had not been hacked away to make streets, and where now is a great gash to let First Street through there was then a breezy, open hill-top, whereon grew brush and wild-flowers. The poppies in those days were eschscholtzias (the learning to spell the name was a feat of my eighth year), and were not subjected to the ignominy of being painted with poinsettias on fringed leather souvenirs for tourists. The yellow violets were gallitas, little roosters, perhaps because in the hands of children they fought to the death, their necks hooked together until one or the other was decapitated. The brodiæas, or wild hyacinths, sometimes now called "rubbernecks," were called cacomites, (four syllables), a word of Aztec origin brought to California by people from Mexico where it was applied to a different flower but one having like this one a sweet edible root.

Between the weeds and bushes there were bare spots of ground where, by careful searching, one might find faint circles about the size of a "two-bit" piece. Wise ones knew that these marked the trap doors of tarantula nests. It was sport to try to pry one open, with mother spider holding it closed. We young vandals would dig out the nests, interested for a moment in the silky lining and the tiny babies and then would throw away the wrecked home of the gorgeous black velvet creatures that did no harm on the open hillside.

At this house Harry and I conducted an extensive "essence factory," collecting old bottles far and near, and filling them with vari-colored liquids, obtained by soaking or steeping different flowers and leaves. We used to drink the brew made from euca-lyptus leaves. The pepper infusion was pale, like tea; that made from old geraniums was of a horrible odor, — hence we liked to inveigle innocent grown folks into smelling it. The cactus solution was thick, like castor oil, and we considered it our most valuable product, having arrived thus early at the notion that difficulty of preparation adds to the cost of a manufactured article.

North of us were several houses containing children — and here I found my first girl playmates — Grace and Susie, Bertha and Eileen. The level street at Court and Hill, protected on three sides by grades too steep for horses, was our safe neighborhood play-ground. I never go through the tunnel that now has pierced the hill without hearing, above the roar of the Hollywood car, the patter of flying feet, the rhythms of the witch dances, the thud-thud of hop-scotch, the shouting boys and girls defending goals in prisoner's base, the old, old song of London Bridge, or the "Intry mintry cutry corn" that determined who was "it" for the twilight game of hide-and-seek — and then the varied-toned bells in the hands of mothers who called the children home.

We played school, jacks, marbles, tag, and an adaptation of *Peck's Bad Boy*, and, between whiles, dolls. Even Harry played with them when we were still youngsters — say eight or nine. He didn't seem young to me then — he was just himself. I called him "Hab." My aunt tells of finding us once about our housekeeping, he doing the doll family washing, and I papering the house. In our menage there was no sex distinction as to the work to be done.

We girls, as we grew older, had a collection of small dolls, none over four inches long, and the various marriages, deaths, and parties kept us busy. I tailored for the whole group, having apparently a talent for trousers, which early experience undoubtedly encouraged me in later life to gather in all the stray pantaloons to cut over into knickerbockers for my numerous boys.

Raids on the Chinese vegetable wagon provided supplies for our cooking over a row of small, outdoor fireplaces we had built in a low bank in our yard. Once my mother was much disturbed to find a little pot of squirrel meat cooking on the stove. She needn't have worried, for I knew as well as she that strychnine, slipped into a small piece of watermelon rind, transferred its evil potency to the body of the little beast that ate it. But it was sport to hang him up as

I had seen the men do at the ranch when butchering a sheep, to skin him and dress the meat, and pretend it was a stew for Isabel, the doll. I had a large collection of squirrel skins tacked up on the barn at the Shepherd house.

After a couple of years we built our own house in the same neighborhood on the southeast corner of Court and Hill Streets. It began as a seven-room cottage, white with green blinds to suit father. Later the roof was raised and a second story inserted and the house painted a more fashionable all-over gray, to suit the ladies.

My mother was a happy woman when, after eleven years of married life, she moved into her very own home. A few months later she suddenly died, leaving my father widowed a second time, a lonely man for the remaining fourteen years of his life.

Mother had never been a strong woman and was unable to withstand an attack of typhus fever, contracted when on an errand of kindliness to a sick and forlorn seamstress. I often wish I might have an adult's knowledge of mother, — my child memories are beautiful. She was tall and slender, with quantities of heavy brown hair, dark eyes, and unusual richness of color in her cheeks which is repeated in some of her grandchildren. It amuses me to recall that I had such absolute faith in her word that on one occasion when she had visited my school and a girl remarked upon what a beautiful mother I had, I stoutly denied the allegation, for had she not herself assured me that she was not pretty?

I suppose that her New England conscience and native modesty could not allow even her little daughter to tell her how lovely she really was. I am told that she "had a knack for clothes" and I remember some of them well enough to confirm the opinion. Her taste allowed beautiful materials and much real lace, but of jewels there were none except some brooches that performed useful service and the wedding and engagement rings that held sentiment.

It was a sad thing that just when her dearest wish, that for her own home, was fulfilled, she must leave it and her three babies for some one else to care for. Fortunately her dearly loved, next-older sister, Martha, was able to take her place.

At the time we built there seemed to be but two styles of architecture in vogue, one square on a four-room base and the other oblong on a six-room plan, the narrow end being to the street, with one tier of rooms shoved back a little in order to provide a small porch, — we chose the latter. Every such house had a bay window in the projecting end, that being the front parlor, and all windows visible from the street must have yellow, varnished inside blinds.

One evening while the building was going on we went over as usual for our daily inspection and noted that the newly set studding marked the coming rooms. The connecting parlors seemed small to our eyes and tastes not yet trained to apartment and bungalow court proportions, so on the following morning father ordered out the wall between proposed front and back parlor, and our large sitting room, — living room it would called today, — was ordained. It was unusual in Los Angeles where the prevailing mode demanded the two parlors. This room was large enough, 18′x33′, to stand the height of the ceiling, fourteen feet. Wide, high double-doors opened into the hall, opposite similar ones into the reception room, giving a feeling of spaciousness to the house.

The furnishing was of necessity more or less that which it is now customary to damn as mid-Victorian, — walnut furniture and a wealth of varying design in carpet, curtains, upholstery, wall-paper; but the whole in this case was kept in harmony by a key color, a medium olive, relieved by soft shades of rose and tan. Even the woodwork was painted to match the ground color of the walls, instead of glistening in the usual glory of varnished redwood or yellow pine. Everything was in good taste except a fearful and wonderful ceiling that was wished on us by the local wallpapering nabob. How fortunate that the walls were so high it was almost out of sight!

Over our heads were the two plaster of Paris centerpieces from which lighting fixtures sprang, first hanging lamps with prismatic fringes, later gas chandeliers. These fruits and flowers were tinted and gilded. Around them was a cream colored sky, set with golden stars, small ones, not planets, — limited in extent by an oval band of brocaded red velvet, this being the pet aversion of Aunt Martha. Outside this pale there was a field of metallic colored paper with an all-over design like chicken wire; next came a border of flowers and something modest to connect the whole artistic creation with the side wall.

We had a ceiling, but there were many things characteristic of the period that we did not have. We never had a "throw," nor a gilded milking stool with a ribbon bow on one leg; we never had a land-scape painted on the stem of a palm leaf, nor oranges on a section of orange wood; we did not hang in any door a portière made of beads, shells, chenille ropes or eucalyptus seeds, all of which things were abroad in the land.

The room contained four bookcases, a rosewood square piano, a large table, a sofa and several easy chairs. From the walls looked down upon us *Pharoah's Horses, The Stag in the Glen,* and the *Drove at the Ford,* (suitable subjects the vogue provided for a family dependent upon livestock), but these were not all, for there were a few reproductions of old masters, a fine portrait of grandfather in his youth, and a picture of the sweet-faced mother who had gone to Heaven, as we children said.

At one end of the room was a white marble mantel with a large grate, always annoying us by its white patchiness in the low toned room, but contributing cheer with the coal fire that, through more than half the year, burned all day long. Los Angeles had no furnaces in those days, but the family was suited by the single fireplace, for one could choose the climate he wished from torrid zone near the grate to arctic in the bay window, where the goldfish circled their watery globe.

The room was the center of a happy family life, where, of an evening, all read by the light of the student lamp, or indulged in games, dominoes, authors, crambo, or logomachy, — sugar-coated ways of getting training respectively in addition, names of books and writers, verse-making and spelling. Father rarely went out, and after the reading of his evening paper might join a lively domino tournament or amuse himself with solitaire.

Until the very last years of his life he busied himself at odd jobs about the house. Sometimes it would be a session with the grandfather clock, sometimes it would be chopping wood. He had the willow brought up from the ranch in long pieces, which he cut and stacked under the house. He raised chickens and at first cared for a horse and cow. Later we kept two horses, dispensed with the cow, and had a man for the livestock and garden and to drive us about town. We did not have a dog regularly but always cats, classical cats. Æneas was very long-legged and Dido lived with us a long time. I think it was she who went every evening with father for his after dinner walk and cigar.

One Thanksgiving time the wagon from the ranch came, bringing us a couple of barrels of apples, a load of wood and a fine turkey for the feast day. Imagine our dismay, one afternoon, to see it mount up on its wings and soar majestically from our hilltop backyard down to the corner of First and Broadway below. He escaped us but, I presume, to some one else he came as a direct answer to prayer.

Father was always interested in flowers and was very successful in making them grow. Usually there was a box of slips out in the back yard. Often he would bring in a rich red Ragged Robin bud, dew-wet, to lay by mother's napkin for breakfast. For himself he put a sprig of lemon-verbena in his button-hole. For some reason, he excepted orange colored flowers from his favor. He made mock of the gay little runners by twisting their name into "nasty-urchins."

The windows of my room, directly over the parlor, were covered with a large, climbing "Baltimore Belle," an old-fashioned small cluster rose that I never see now-a-days. From my side window I looked out on a long row of blue-blossomed agapanthus, interspersed with pink belladonnas, flowers that in summer repeated the blue of the mountains touched at sunset with pink lights.

Every night when ready for bed, I opened the inside blinds and looked at the mountains and up to the stars and enlarged my heart, for what can give one the sense of awe and beauty that the night sky does?

The location of our home on the brow of a hill was chosen because of the view and the sense of air and space. Below us was the little city, the few business blocks, the homes set in gardens on tree shaded streets, the whole surrounded by orchards and vineyards. On clear days we could see the mountains far in the east and the ocean at San Pedro, with Santa Catalina beyond.

One very rainy winter, possibly '86, we watched the flood waters from the river creep up Aliso Street and into Alameda: we saw bridges go out and small houses float down stream. Then it was that Martin Aguierre, a young policeman, won the admiration of everyone when he rode his black horse into the torrent and rescued flood victims from floating houses and debris in mid-stream. One of the girls in my room at school lost all her clothing except what she wore, and we had a "drive" for our local flood-sufferer.

This was a very different river in summer. I once saw a woman whose nerves had been wracked by dangerous winter fordings when the water swirled about the body of the buggy, get out of her carriage, letting it ford the Los Angeles river while she stepped easily across the entire stream. She had a complex, but she didn't know that name for her fear!

Beyond the river and up the hill on the other side stood, stark and lonely, the "Poor House," the first unit of the present General Hospital. Many a time when the skies forbore to rain I had it pointed out to me as my probable ultimate destination; for, after the bad middle years of the seventies when to a general financial depression was added a pestilence that killed off all the lambs, and to that was added a disastrous investment in mines, the firm of Flint, Bixby & Co. was sadly shaken, and it was of great moment whether or not sufficient moisture should come to provide grass and grain for the stock. So, if the sun shone too constantly and the year wore on to Christmas without a storm the ominous words, "a dry year," were heard and the bare building across the river loomed menacingly. But it always rained in time to save us!

Rain and overflowing rivers connote mud. Walkers on the cement sidewalks beside our paved streets little realize what wonderful mud was lost when Progress covered our adobe. With its first wetting it became very slippery on top of a hard base, but as more water fell and it was kneaded by feet and wheels, it became first like well-chewed gum and then a black porridge. I have seen signs that warned against drowning in the bog in the business center of town. An inverted pair of boots sticking out of a pile of mud in front of the old Court House once suggested that a citizen had gone in head first and disappeared.

Small boys turned an honest nickel or two by providing plank foot-bridges or selling individual "crickets" which the wayfarer might take with him from corner to corner. As the sun came out and the mud thickened the streets became like monstrous strips of sticky fly paper. We walked the cobblestone gutters until our rubbers were in shreds, or, when necessity drove us into the gum, lost them.

A friend assures me that one Sunday morning she set out for a church near the center of the city, that she made slow progress for a block and a half, and then, realizing that so much time had passed that she could not arrive in time for service, turned around and went home. It had taken her an hour and a half to make the round trip amounting to three blocks.

There is no mud so powerful when it is in its prime as adobe, and when it dries in all its trampled ridges and hollows, it is as hard as a rock. It takes all summer to wear it down level, ready to begin over again with the new rains. There are a few places yet, where, some rainy day if you are feeling extra fit, you may try a stroll across a Los Angeles street and learn to sympathize with a captured fly.

Certain other interesting kinds of soil are also covered up in Los Angeles. On the southwest corner of Temple and Broadway there is mica cropping out between the strata, and up by Court Street Angel's Flight there is a nice white formation very like chalk. I liked to cut it into odd shapes.

CHAPTER XI

More About Los Angeles

I AM still a person somewhat young and lively who has had the strange experience of seeing barley fields sprout houses like the magic soldiers from the sowing of dragon's teeth; of finding cactus and gravel and sage turned overnight into leagues of orange trees; of watching my little city multiply itself a hundred fold. What wonder that I cannot forbear to talk about it, to tell of how once upon a time the street of sky-scrapers was a shaded way before a few rose-covered cottages, or how the hills of Hollywood were bare brown velvet beyond the vacant fields that lay west of Figueroa Street, itself unfinished. When we looked over the town from our home on the Court Street hill we saw a place of trees and cottages, of open spaces and encircling groves. Only to our left were business houses, and they neither high nor imposing. On Pound Cake Hill, where now the County Court House rises, was the square, two-storied high school building, which a few years later crossed Temple Street on stilts, and went over to its new abiding place on California Street.

Just below us was the old jail, enclosed by its high white fence which may have shut in prisoners and shut out the curious who approached on Franklin Street, but whose secrets were wide open to the sky. Once our whole backyard and the top of our chicken house and barn were black with men strangely eager to look down upon a fellow man whom we, the public, were hanging high upon a gallows within that old stockade. We children were shut in the house and did not see, but the next day my small brother and another tiny boy were found trying to hang each other.

The jail was in the rear of the city buildings, a row of low adobes on Spring Street, opposite the old court house, the one built by John Temple. Nearby, the post-office occupied the first floor of the new I. O. O. F. building, a little too far south to be sure, — nearly to First Street, — but perhaps the spaciousness and freshness compensated for its distance from the business center to the north.

Across the way from it there stood a small white cottage, with a hedge of cypress and a lawn. My first school was around the corner in a similar white house, and on my way home I was permitted to stop and get our mail from our box at the post-office.

The shopping district ran from this "civic center" up to the Plaza, the very region that is now being retrieved for the heart of the public life of Los Angeles city and county.

Not long ago I discovered, stranded high on the front wall of an old brick building, the abandoned sign of "The Queen," the store from which came my "pebble-goat" school shoes, the store itself long ago having followed the shoes "to the bone yard."

In Temple Block were many offices, but I remember it as the abode of Godfrey, the photographer, who, plentifully supplied with red velvet fringed chairs and pronged head braces, took the pictures of the Angeleños.

Over in the Downey Block, where now the U.S. Government Building stands, and in the buildings to the north, were some of our most frequented stores, among them Meyberg's Crystal Palace, a source of china and glassware, and Dotter and Bradley, whose furniture firm later took the name of Los Angeles Furniture Co. A little Barker store was born over near First and Spring, but that was so far from the center of things, and chilly and lonely, that it moved nearer to the Plaza, — and now Barker Brothers aspires to be the largest furniture "emporium" in the world with a palace on Seventh Street.

I knew something of Commercial and Los Angeles Streets as business thoroughfares, but their importance was passing, and the new Baker Block was the last word in elegance, and the pride of all the dwellers in Los Angeles. Here Rev. B. F. Coulter opened a dry-goods store that continues to this day in the fourth location that I remember, moving first to Second and Spring, then following the fashion up to Broadway and later going to Seventh. Then as now this establishment specialized in blankets, perhaps because Mr. Coulter had a woolen mill over the hill near the present corner of Figueroa and Fifth Streets. The old brick walls of this factory may still be seen — the main part of a modern-fronted garage. There was a little stream there that was called Los Reyes, — the Kings, — rather a humble place for royalty in a city of the Queen of the Angels.

Two favorite shops of that time have disappeared, that of Dillon and Kennealy, who carried a line of most lovely linens from their

Irish homeland, and the City of Paris, "the best place for lace and trimmings," I used to hear. That was before the time of ready-made clothing, and real ladies were most particular about the quality of materials used and the nicety of workmanship.

One day a small new store, with a fifty-foot frontage, appeared at the corner of Temple and Spring. It was called the Boston Store — reminiscent of the Boston ships upon which the early California ladies depended for all their finery. Good shoppers soon recognized high-grade materials and efficient salesmanship, and the firm had to move a few doors south to obtain larger space, and then, made bold by public favor, it went pioneering way out among the residences on Broadway near Third, to remain a few years until it set the fashion of Seventh Street, — J. W. Robinson & Co.

Mrs. Ponet supplied the ladies with bonnets, when Miss Daley didn't, and Mr. Ponet framed our pictures and buried our dead.

As I was only a little girl in those days, I do not know so much about the shopping habits of the gentlemen, but I remember that they bought hats from D. Desmond, cutlery from C. Ducommun and watches and jewels from S. Nordlinger.

Not long ago I picked up an old map of Los Angeles showing a new subdivision just west of Figueroa. The map was issued by Stoll and Thayer, who with Hellman, Stassforth Co., were the chief purveyors of school books, slates, Christmas cards with silk fringe, lace paper valentines and other necessities. Here I bought those classics, McGuffy's Fourth Reader, Robinson's Arithmetic, Harper's Geography, and Collier and Daniel's Latin Book.

For years it was necessary for anyone desiring a book other than those standard works known to druggists and stationers to send away for it, so it was a great thing for lovers of literature when Mr. C. C. Parker came to town and opened a book shop for books only, — no twine or glue or notebooks or cosmetics or toys, not even text books admitted to his shelves.

Over east of the shopping district lay Chinatown, at one time a very interesting and picturesque part of Los Angeles, having a least 7,000 inhabitants, but owing to the Exclusion Act of the nineties now dwindled to 2,000. With its going has come a distinct loss in color, to say nothing of the much regretted race of competent and loyal household servants.

There used to be three joss houses, or Chinese temples, and a theatre with a large troupe of players, including a lady star, a rarity, as usually all the actors are men. There was weird music to be heard, there were feasts and fortune tellers and funerals where the chief figure was rushed at break-neck speed to the cemetery, followed by a spring wagon load of food while loyal friends scattered bits of paper to distract attention of the devil in his pursuit of the newly dead.

But the life was not all picturesque. There were slave women and tong wars and murders and individual persecutions of Chinese by low grade whites, and ever the haunting memory of the massacre of 1871 when nineteen Chinese lost their lives at the hands of a mob.

The changing of prestige of hotels has marked the changing city. Just now the Biltmore holds the center of the stage, last year it was the Ambassador, once it was the Bella Union, perhaps the most interesting of them all, dating as it did, back into pueblo days. The Pico House of the early seventies prided itself on rivalling the San Francisco hostelries, but before a decade had passed it had to yield first place to the St. Elmo, the place chosen in which to do honor to Mrs. Hayes, the wife of the President. I have personal memories of both the Pico and the St. Elmo. In the first we once stayed several days during one of my earliest trips to Los Angeles, and in the second I climbed the red velveted stairs, holding my mother's hand to greet the chief lady of the land. The poor old place is now a ten-cent lodging house, just north of the post-office.

When the Nadeau was completed, towering four stories and containing all the latest wrinkles, among them the first local elevator, it easily assumed first place, but in such a bustling, booming town it soon had to pass the favor on to the Hollenbeck; then came the Westminster and the Van Nuys, which I believe still clings to a little back-water distinction.

The sudden end of the boom about eighty-seven had one very excellent result, it saved us the chagrin of having our finest caravanserie called Hotel Splendid — it never got beyond the foundations, out at Tenth and Main. Perhaps the name was no worse than San Francisco's Palace which has built about itself such a tradition that no one stops to consider the self-assumption of its designation.

During those boom years Los Angeles was having its first experience of rapid growth, and we were almost as proud and boastful then as we are now, — at least in quality if not in quantity. It seemed just as exciting to suddenly grow from ten to fifty thousand, as it does to aim at a million or two. We hadn't invented the name realtor for our land sellers or established courses at college in realtoring, but there were already enterprising boosters. One of them displayed in his office window this hospitable biblical text: "I was a stranger and ye took me in."

It was during that period that we boldly discarded gas as a means of lighting our streets and adopted electricity, the first city in the land to do it. How imposing were our six tall poles each carrying four arc lights, four substitute moons, protected by a little tin umbrella. What strange and beautiful blue light filtered through our windows, making on the walls black shadows of the swaying eucalyptus branches like Japanese silhouettes.

The summer that we first had these wonder lanterns the very sky put on a nightly pageant of color, most gorgeous sunsets to celebrate our progress, and incidentally to mark the fact that the upper air was full of a fine ash from a volcanic eruption in far away Java.

I wonder what we could do now if the railroads should start another rate war as they did when the Santa Fe first came into Southern California. Tickets from the middle west dropped to five dollars, and on one day went down to one. We would need a host of Aladdins with obedient genii to build in a minute not palaces but just plain houses and schools, — the fact is that one or two such magic builders would not at all be despised by our present boards of education.

I have spoken of stores and public buildings and hotels and real estate offices but they were not all that the streets afforded; there was a barber shop where father and I got our respective hairs cut, accepting the fragrant offering of bay rum, supposed to ward off head colds due to the exposure of lightening one's head covering, but refusing emphatically the hair oil in the pink, brass-nozzled bottle. Then there was the fruit stand next to Wollacott's Wholesale Liquor Establishment near the post-office where we bought the ceremonial bananas that completed the barbering, bananas at five cents apiece. If none could be found a like amount was invested in sugary peppermint drops. These delicacies were eaten at the little Wells Fargo office on the east side of Temple block where there was time enough and little enough doing for Mr. Pridham and father to tilt back their round chairs and have a good gossip.

One day we went over to investigate the crowd that had gathered on the covered sidewalk in front of the Baker Block on North Main Street. Suddenly a man came balancing across the tight rope that was stretched above us. I saw him stop there over our open-mouthed heads and flip a flap-jack in the pan he carried. I do not know why he thus showed his prowess nor what his reward, but he furnished a

passing entertainment for the inhabitants of Los Angeles back in
the later seventies, and his ghost still walks in mid-air for me
whenever I go through that old part of town.

His is not the only walking spirit. There in the Plaza still stands
the shade of the peripatetic dentist, fore-runner of Painless Parker,
who once stood for several days in a red and gold chariot containing
a gorgeous, throne-like chair; for a consideration he pulled teeth
of any who were in search of relief.

Still a third ghost walks and calls in unforgotten accents, "Ice
Cream," the white-clad Mexican, Nicholás Martinez, who went
about the town with a freezer on his head, and in his hand a circular
tin carrier, with a place for spoons in the middle and holes for the
six tumblers in which he served his wares. There was a great scurrying for nickels among the children when his cry was heard in the
land.

In those days two street car lines meandered, the one way out to
Agricultural Park (Exposition), a large bare space with a few old
eucalyptus trees, and the grand stand beside the race-track; the
other south on Spring to Fifth, up Fifth to Olive and around the
corner of the park to Sixth, and then up to Pearl, the name of
Figueroa Street, north of Pico where the bend is. Each line boasted
two cars so that simultaneous trips in opposite directions were possible. The cars were very small and drawn by mules; there was no
separate conductor; we put our tickets — bought at the neighboring drug store — into a glass box near the door. It is told that on
the Main Street line it was the custom for the driver on late trips
to stop the car, wind the reins around the brake handles, and escort
lone lady passengers to their front doors, — so much for leisure
and gallantry in old Los Angeles. Even as late as 1890 the car once
waited while Katherine Carr ran into Mott's market for her meat!

Sometimes we took the car for Sixth and Pearl and then walked
on down to Twelfth, where Aunt Margaret lived for a time. The
street was a grass-bordered road and along the west side the foot-
path followed a *zanja* (a ditch for water). Mr. H. K. W. Bent,
the postmaster, and a man who was in every way a value to the
community, had an orange grove here and lived in it. As I passed it
I would meditate, not on his high position, (he was my Sunday
School superintendent), but on the strange thing I had heard about
him. He ate pie for breakfast! That was undoubtedly a taste
brought straight from New England. We happened to import a
different one; we had doughnuts twice a day every day in the year.

His taste, being different was queer. I guess each family had beans and brown bread at least once a week, with frequent meals of boiled codfish, attended by white sauce and pork scraps.

The trip on the other line was out past vineyards, an occasional house, one of them being the adobe mistakenly called the head-quarters of General Fremont, far, far away to the race-track, to see our Silverheel trot. This old adobe road house had been named in honor of General Fremont although it was far from the center of town where he had stayed during the exciting period of the American conquest and was not built until some years later.

We seldom had a chance to see any good horse race and then only as a concession to the fathers, for races were frowned upon by mothers as being unsuitable for Christians and girls.

The circus, however, was not under the ban, and "joy was unconfined" when we heard the shrill calliope in the streets and saw the line of elephants and caged lions and gay horsewomen filing along Spring Street. There were usually enough children in the family to provide excuses for all the men-folk who longed to attend the show as chaperones. Grandfather felt that seventy years of abstinence justified him in examining a circus thoroughly and Harry was his lucky escort, when, with his inhibitions released, he visited everything, even to the last side-show.

After a full-fledged Barnum and Bailey the small tent on the lot now graced by the Times building where trained horses and dogs performed for a month was too tame for the gentlemen, but afforded pleasure to the children.

Once Los Angeles was small enough to be very happy during county fair week, with its races and shows of fine stock and the usual indoor exhibits of fruits and grains, its fancy work and jellies, and then the fair developed into orange shows and flower festivals and finally into the fiesta. We lined the streets with palms and decked the buildings with the orange, red and green banners and played and paraded for a week in April, the peak of Spring. We saw our red-shirted firemen with their flower-garlanded, shining engines, drawn by those wisest of animals, the fire horses; bands played, Spanish cavaliers and señoritas appeared again in our midst, marvellous floats vied for first prize — gay days.

Who that saw the many-footed dragon that wound its silken, glistening way out of Chinatown into our streets can ever forget its beauty? Or the floats that carried the bewitching little Chinese children wearing their vivid embroidered garments and beaded head-dresses? Alas, they are buried now in their American cover-alls and corduroys.

What happened to us? Did we grow too unwieldy, or too sophis-ticated or were we swamped with midwest sobriety? We gave our parade to Pasadena, who put it in wintry January instead of fra-grant, flowering April; San Bernardino has the orange show, fiesta has disappeared altogether. But I have heard whispers that indicate that mayhap the spirit of pageantry and frolic is about to return to Los Angeles. (It does this 1931!)

Many changes have come but each phase as it exists seems the natural condition; the old days that I have been recalling were the "Now" that we knew. In the past there was less hurry and more room in our streets that were built to be but ways between cottage homes where now and then a wagon or carriage might go. How-ever, there were no more hours a day to fill or dispose of than we have now. We could stroll down the street to do our errands, meet-ing friends at every turn; we could drive if preferred, and although Harry Horse and the phaeton made slower progress than Henry Ford or Lionel Limousin, he did not have so far to go and he could stand as long as he wished before the shop door, so that the time consumed by my lady was no more than in these days of suburban homes, and parking places far, far from where she really wants to go.

In the matters of health, friendship, intelligence, the number of inhabitants in a city are of little moment; happiness does not in-crease with population.

I find it interesting, however, to have in my mind pictures of the little vanished village that once was Los Angeles. I also find it in-teresting to watch its present turmoil and energy and to speculate on its future; to see signs of intellectual, artistic and social vitality that exist among the scattered groups and individuals now pouring into this seething community; to wonder how soon the wheels of progress are going to stop rattling long enough for us to hear our-selves think, catch our breath and develop some sort of cohesive social organism.

It is the fashion just now to make a butt of Los Angeles, to see only its obsessions, its crudities, its banalities. Those who really com-prehend the amazing number of people daily crowding in upon us, and remember that the bulk of the people are inevitably strangers to each other, each ready to shift responsibility to someone sup-posedly an older citizen, cannot but have patience, cannot but rejoice in the really fine things that have been done and are doing.

CHAPTER XII

The Back Country and The Admiral

Fᴏʀ seventy years after its founding in 1781, Los Angeles was the only pueblo, as distinguished from presidio or mission, in the southern part of this state; and until the sudden growth of San Francisco during the gold excitement, it was the largest city in California, boasting about twenty-five hundred inhabitants when it came under American rule. Of the three neighboring missions, San Gabriel and San Juan Capistrano antedate Los Angeles by a few years, while San Fernando was founded about twelve years later.

During the Spanish and Mexican regimes California's population was largely scattered upon the ranchos, and this condition remained for nearly a generation after the settlement of the northern counties. The story of the life in this grazing land is familiar, — the story of its leisureliness and hospitality; of its life on horseback, of the great herds of black, lean, long-horned cattle, the offspring of the few animals brought in by the padres; of the devotion of the founders of the missions, of their prosperity and then of their decline under the secularization of the Mexican law. Even as late as the time of my childhood the country was still very empty and Los Angeles was a little city set in gardens and orchards, a narrow border of cultivated lands separating it from the wide, almost treeless, valley.

An exception to this general condition was the district to the East, centering about San Gabriel; this old mission early won the title Queen of the Missions, not because of the size or beauty of church or location, but because of the large number of Indians under its care, and the extent of its herds, orchards, vineyards and grainfields. Its cattle, estimated variously from 75,000 to a 100,000, roamed the great valley even to the foot of the mountains San Gorgonio and San Jacinto; for convenience in administration a branch, or *asistencia*, was established at San Bernardino in 1810.

The San Gabriel vineyard numbered a hundred and fifty thousand vines, from cuttings brought from Spain, and the making of wine and brandy (aguardiente) became an important industry. Its orchards, at their peak, contained over twenty-three hundred trees, most of them oranges, which the padres introduced, together with olives, pomegranates, and lemons. The gardens were surrounded with adobe walls or cactus hedges as a protection against marauding cattle or people, who, as one padre once quaintly said, "put out the hand too often."

The first San Gabriel oranges were planted in 1804 by Padre Tomas Sanchez. Thirty years afterward the earliest grove in Los Angeles was set out by Don Luis Vignes, to be followed in 1841 by that of William Wolfskill, whose orchard later became famous as the largest in the United States. He was instrumental in bringing in many new plants to this country, and the beauty of his home place was great. His gardens gave way for the Southern Pacific Arcade Station, his orchard ground is covered by the city's business, and no one thinks of Los Angeles as once the actual center of California's orange growing industry.

And as these groves have been supplanted by the houses of trade, the Mission's orchards have been transformed into homes. But when I was a little girl they still remained, had even been extended by those who came into possession after the secularization of San Gabriel.

Many of the names now familiar around Pasadena were the names of these estates. For instance, San Marino and Oak Knoll were the properties of Don Benito (Benjamin) Wilson, and his son-in-law, J. De Barth Shorb. Wilson was one of those Americans who came here during the Mexican rule, married into an old California family, and became identified with the land. It is for him that the astronomical peak is named, because it was he who at the expense of much money and labor built the trail to the top of the ridge. He had hopes of finding timber suitable for making of casks for his wine, but although he failed in this there was some lumber brought down on burro back.

I believe Mr. Wilson was also responsible for naming Big Bear Valley, — since the building of the dam, Big Bear Lake. Soon after his arrival in California he led an expedition through the San Bernardino mountains in chase of some Indians who had been raiding cattle and horses in the lowlands. There were many bears in the mountain valley and over twenty were killed at this time, each one being lassoed by two men in the California fashion.

Another familiar name is El Molino, the old mill which the

mission built. It fell into disrepair, but was rescued by Col. Kewen, who made of it a charming home, while developing an estate about it. The story of Mrs. Kewen's five hundred callas for Easter decorations at the Episcopal Church has come down. Calla lilies were in better repute then than now.

Mrs. Albert Sidney Johnston called her new home in California Fair Oaks, the name of her Virginian birthplace. Los Robles (The Oaks), was the home of Governor Stoneman.

Old timers will recall the estate of L. J. Rose, Sunny Slope, famous both for its wines and brandies and for its stables of fine horses. Major Truman in his book, *Semi-tropical California*, dating from 1874, speaks of this district as a "fruit belt, two miles wide and ten miles long," and calls it the California Lombardy.

It was just next door to this region of wine and brandy that the temperance people from Indiana started their colony on a portion of the old San Pasqual grant, the ranch where Flint, Bixby & Co. had pastured their sheep after the desert crossing in 1854. This colony devoted itself to oranges, not so intoxicating as grapes, and gave the name of the chief industry to the fashionable avenue. After a time they began to call themselves Pasadena, an imported name, and after a little more time we in Los Angeles began to know about the new settlement which was getting big enough to maintain a modest daily stage to the city, — a spring wagon. The road followed much the same route as is used today, down across the unbridged Arroyo Seco and over the flowery field that later became Garvanza, a field filled in spring with great masses of wild blossoms, poppies, and lupine, larkspur, tidy-tips, and pink owl-clover, — pink tassels we children called them; past the Sycamores, once a popular country beer-garden, now a city park, through the little settlement known as East Los Angeles, along Buena Vista Street (North Broadway), so called because of its attractive outlook across the early gardens and orchards of Los Angeles, and on into the Plaza. The earliest name for this street was Calle de Eternidad — Eternity Street — because it was the road to the cemetery.

One of the places reached by this road was the hill near the point on the brink of the Arroyo where ostriches now congregate, which was a favorite place for the city picnickers, — far away when measured by hay wagon speed and untouched by any "improvements." It was there one spring day that my schoolmates and I, of that grade which studies American colonial history, acted out a recent lesson, "storming the heights of Abraham" up the steep hillside, pushing our way under the oaks, through brush, past great clumps of maiden-hair fern to the mesa atop where we found a million seeming butterflies, the mariposa lilies, hovering over the grass.

While Pasadena was growing up to the west of the old district, "Lucky" Baldwin was developing on the east that loveliest of all oak-clad ranches, the Santa Anita, and making of it a show place sought by the few hardy and intrepid tourists who were beginning to find their way into Southern California, making a name for it far and wide not only because of its beauty but because of his famous racing stables.

Beyond that there wasn't much that a child would even hear of, — there was a ranch at Duarte and another called Azusa, and then far to the east, across foothills covered with sage and cactus, and mighty "washes" filled with granite boulders was Cucamonga Ranch with its old winery and vineyard, planted sometime in the forties by members of the Lugo family from the Rancho Santa Ana del Chino, across the valley. I understand that Chino means curly and relates to the character of the locks of an early owner. This ranch was under the management of Isaac Williams, a son-in-law of old Don Antonio Maria Lugo, the man who at one time held leagues and leagues of land all the way from San Pedro to San Bernardino. For many years it was a most hospitable way-station for all travelers from over the plains to Los Angeles. At the time when my father came through the Chino supported ten thousand head of cattle, half as many horses and thirty-five thousand New Mexican sheep. What it was twenty-five years later I do not know, but the hey-day of the ranches was over and the new town had not yet come.

In the far eastern end of the valley was the old town of San Bernardino, so named probably because it was on that Saint's day that the padres established their *asistencia*. With the downfall of the missions this early development was stopped, moreover the troubles with "wild" Indians were greater here than in localities further from the mountain passes. The present town dates from 1851 when a company of Mormons, about four hundred strong, came across the deserts and mountains from Salt Lake City, and purchasing a portion of the San Bernardino Ranch from the Lugos, rapidly put a large acreage under cultivation.

This ranch was owned by three young Lugos and their cousin, Diego Sepulveda, whose granddaughter, Mrs. Florence Schone-

man, tells me that they were delighted to sell and get a chance to
move nearer the center of life at Los Angeles and consequently
made the easiest terms with the colonists — something like $500
down and the balance to be paid after crops began to bring in returns.

Before long these thrifty settlers were shipping vegetables, flour
and dairy products into Arizona and to Los Angeles, a three-day
haul away. Their flour was ground in the mill built by Louis Rubidoux, who had purchased a portion of the neighboring Jurupa grant
from Don Juan Bandini, to whom the grant had been made a year
or two after the time he was traveling down the coast aboard the
sail ship whereon Richard H. Dana was spending his two years
before the mast. Louis Rubidoux, whose name is kept in mind by
the mountain that guards the entrance to the modern Riverside, was
a Frenchman, a native of St. Louis, who had come to California in
1840 by way of New Mexico. He was a cultivated man and a successful rancher who later became interested in cutting up his land
into smaller holdings and has the name of being the first "sub-
divider" of Southern California, the one who set the fashion that
has of late grown to such appalling proportions.

The beginnings of Riverside were made in 1870 when a colony
of people from various places in the East bought some of this bench
land above the Santa Ana River. Although the first plan was to go
into the cultivation of the silk-worm for which there was a great
enthusiasm for a year or two, even to the extent of generous
bounties offered by the State legislature, it was not long before
the town was in its characteristic groove; by the time we had moved
to Los Angeles the first naval orange had fruited and the first
Glenwood Inn offered a setting for hospitality, — Riverside, oranges, tourists! But I knew nothing about it. Why should I? It
was far away and very small, so far in fact that its inhabitants,
according to a local history, allowed a week for a trip to Los Angeles and return. At first they had to drive all the way but after a
few years there was a railroad extending toward them as far as
Uncle Billy Rubottom's. And who now knows where that was? It
wasn't Pomona, which then was barely in embryo, being represented by the few settlers under the San José Hills on the properties
belonging to the Palomares, the Vejar and the Phillips families,
but Spadra. Uncle Billy had come to California from Spadra
Bluffs in Arkansas and to the very popular way-station for the
Butterfield stages which he maintained he gave the old home name.

Going on toward the city one crossed the Puente Ranch and came
to El Monte, which doesn't mean anything about mountains, but
refers to the thickets of willows that even today are characteristic of
the place. "The Monte" it used to be called when first it was
founded, a little later than San Bernardino, by people who came in
from Texas. Although now this town retains characteristics that
might make it seem of Mexican origin it was in its beginnings
entirely an American settlement. It was chosen for its good farm
lands, and soon its citizens were making a success raising corn,
melons, pumpkins, and hogs, and judging from the records of
early chroniclers, rather strenuous boys who seemed ever ready to
join with Los Angeles in the wild doings that marked those days
after the gold excitement had brought to California multitudes of
the bad as well as of the good.

Anaheim was the next town to be founded, following in 1857,
the Los Angeles of 1781, and the two of 1851, San Bernardino and
El Monte. After that the impulse for the starting of new communities gained headway, not so fast during the sixties, but the
seventies marked the beginning of many now prosperous places and
the booming eighties brought to birth many a city (some of them
still-born).

Anaheim was projected by a group of San Francisco Germans
who went about its making in a characteristically methodical and
thrifty way. So far as I can discover it never went through the
agonies of hope and despair that so often mark the course of utopian
schemes for co-operative settlement.

The method adopted for its beginning was to purchase upward
of eleven hundred acres, send an agent ahead who attended to the
clearing off of the sage and cactus, the division of the land into
twenty-acre portions, ten acres of each being set out to vines, and to
the laying out of lots in the center for the necessary shops, school,
post-office, etc. When all was ready the colonists came in a body,
finding everything prepared for them.

One of the first things that had been done was the development
of an intricate irrigation system, tapping the Santa Ana River for
water. This made an oasis of the colony during the terrible droughts
that came a few years later. The edges of the zanjas had been
planted with willows and cottonwoods and all about the settlement
was a palisade of willow stakes, which, set in the damp soil, speedily
sprouted and formed a leafy barrier to the thousands of desperate,
starving cattle, which but for this defense, would have overrun the
one green spot in all the country round.

Speaking of sprouting willows recalls the story that the first settlers in El Monte made rough bedsteads in their dirt floored houses from the native wood and that shortly the posts put forth branches and made each bed a bower.

The people at Anaheim were able almost at once to ship grapes to the San Francisco market, and also were soon making a very good wine for similar export. They made use of a neighboring small harbor which soon came to be known as Anaheim Landing. Recently my Aunt Margaret told me that the first wool that they sent to San Francisco from the Cerritos went from this place instead of from San Pedro as it did later.

In 1876 a group of idealistic Polish gentlefolk under the leadership of Madame Helena Modjeska and her husband, Count Bozenta, and including Henryk Sienkiewicz, came to Anaheim and started a small colony in a neighboring cañon. Like many another dream it did not meet the hopes of the dreamers. It was then that Madame Modjeska set about learning English and returned to the stage, winning great honor and success in her adopted country. After about two years Mr. Sienkiewicz returned to Poland, wrote *Quo Vadis* and the succession of novels which have given him a world-wide fame.

The success of Anaheim led to the founding in following years of other colonies and towns. Westminster, Santa Ana, Tustin were small centers to which I occasionally had the privilege of driving with my elders on business bent. And I should not forget Gospel Swamp — home of camp-meetings, whose choice name may have contributed to its early demise.

Downey, named for the popular governor, was nearer our ranch and even in those days attracted visitors by an agricultural fair. I recall a dusty trip over there to observe my only namesake, a Holstein bossy, winning a blue ribbon, — Sally, and her twin brother, who bore the name of my beloved cousin, Harry.

Compton to me was an established fact but to the ranch dwellers it was a new Methodist place offering them the conveniences of a nearby post-office, church and physician. How well I remember Dr. Whaley, whose practices had not been tempered by a breath of homœopathy. When I had so bad a cold I couldn't celebrate getting to be seven years old by the promised picnic at the beach, nor wear my bulky new bathing suit made of heavy navy blue flannel and trimmed with three rows of white tape, he was called to cure me. This he proceeded to do by swabbing my throat with thick yellow stuff with iron in it, by giving a black dose that necessitated the immediate cleaning of my teeth lest it rot them, and by ordering the application of a strong, large mustard plaster, first to my front, then to my back, then to each side, thus making a complete red jacket of burns about my body. Apparently it cured me. It is strange how popular mustard was in those days, not only the terrible plasters but the torturing foot baths for colds — boiling water reinforced by that awful stinging powder that came out of yellow covered cans bearing the lion and unicorn of old England. I wonder if doctors and parents applied the cure to themselves as well as to children.

Compton was the second stop beyond Cerritos on the wonderful railroad from Wilmington to Los Angeles; the first was Dominguiz and the third was Florence and that was all until one reached Alameda Street, and the "depot'" which was on a corner by a flour mill. What fun it was to go to the city! We got into the carriage in the courtyard, and drove out through the gates and down the hill to the river, where sometimes the fording was very exciting, — water might come into the buggy if it was winter and had been raining a long time; then there were two separate "willows" to go through, only a half-mile ride in all. Either we were always very prompt or the train was not, for there was time and permission to put our ears down on the rail to listen for the coming train, and there was a low trestle over the "slew" where we might walk the ties.

I was amused to read recently in an old book the boast that Los Angeles was a railroad center, the focus for four roads! This one that I knew was the first, twenty-three miles in length; next was the one to Spadra, longest of all, thirty miles; then one to San Fernando, reaching out through the grain fields of the valley twenty-two miles toward San Francisco, and the Anaheim road, twenty-eight miles. Progress had arrived.

From the beginnings of Los Angeles and San Gabriel, San Pedro was the port, but for very many years it remained the desolate spot that is described in *Two Years Before the Mast*. There was one hide house to which, when a boat came into port, the accumulated stores of hides and tallow were hauled. These products which the inhabitants exchanged with Yankee traders for everything they needed or wanted in the way of manufactured goods, did not require very elaborate facilities, and it was the custom to roll the bundles over the cliffs to the rocks below where the sailors must gather them up and carry on their heads out to their boats. The sailors also must carry over the rough trail to the top of the bluff the boxes and barrels containing their merchandise. San Pedro was not a popular port. But conditions must have improved very soon after the visits of Dana, for there is extant a letter from the Angeleño of Boston origin, Abel Stearns, in which he tells of his notion to improve the situation. He took up a collection among his friends, to the amount of one hundred and fifty dollars, secured the services of some mission Indians and in a few weeks had made the first road down to water level.

After the admission of California as a state, travel to and from Los Angeles increased and before long stages between San Pedro and the city became necessary. Don David Alexander and General Phineas Banning were the prime movers who developed this. Gen. Banning is one of the most picturesque figures of the early American period and was very active in every field of the development of transportation. At one time he was doing a large business freighting supplies over the Mormon trail to Salt Lake City and the territory beyond. And he was largely responsible for the building of that first railway, the San Pedro-Los Angeles, an improvement which put an end to the exciting stage races that introduced to their future home both those chroniclers of early days, Harris Newmark and Horace Bell — wild rides to a wilder community. People today sometimes deplore a "crime wave," but to live up to the proportions set in 1853 Los Angeles should stage about four hundred murders a day every day in the year, for that year there was an average of more than one killing a day in a population of about twenty-five hundred.

It was in 1858, I believe, that Gen. Banning promoted the town New San Pedro, later naming it for his birthplace in Delaware, Wilmington. Here he built his home and planted the garden that remains today. I remember going there once as a child with my mother to call upon Mrs. Banning and seeing out among the flowers a most lovely little girl named Lucy—whose later beauty is a Los Angeles tradition.

During the time of the Civil War the Government established Drum Barracks in Wilmington, thus adding to its importance, and it was one of the government warehouses, later abandoned, which was bought for the Alamitos ranch, taken down, moved the ten miles over to the ranch and rebuilt, where it can still be seen by motorists passing over the Anaheim Road, a great red barn with white trimmings.

A forgotten fact about Wilmington is that it was the home of

Wilson College, the gift of Don Benito to the Southern Metho-
dists, and though short-lived, was the fore-runner of such institutions as the University of Southern California, Occidental, and
Pomona. This college was housed in two of the buildings of the deserted Drum Barracks.

I have numerous memories of Wilmington, for it was there that
my Uncle John and Aunt Susan set up housekeeping, and lived until they moved over to the Alamitos. From this port I once took
steamer with my parents for San Francisco, and received one of the
most unexpected experiences of my life, the sudden onset of sea-
sickness as the steamer rounded Point Firmin. I was at dinner with
father, enjoying an ear of corn.

I also remember a Christmas tree at the church from which Santa
Claus handed me a little covered sewing box. This must have been
the church which in its beginnings had so few attendants that there
was only one member who could sing at all, (Aunt Margaret told
me), "Prophet" Potts; and as he knew but one hymn, every Sunday the service contained "Coronation."

Aunt Margaret used to tell another church story also. Soon after
she first came to Cerritos there was an attempt to organize a Congregational church in Los Angeles. The community approved, and
although there were but six actual members, the minister and his
wife, the deacon and his wife, Mrs. Mary Scott and Mrs. Jotham
Bixby, many other citizens contributed towards it and a lot was
secured on the west side of New High Street near Temple and a
building was put up. Everything now was complete and the day of
dedication approached. The visiting minister from San Francisco
came down by boat to Wilmington and was met by the Bixbys and
taken over to the Cerritos for the night. The next day they all drove
the sixteen miles to the city to go to church. Aunt Margaret noticed
a certain constraint in the air and a black eye on the minister. After
service she discovered that the afternoon before the minister and
the deacon had gotten into a fist fight in the furniture store over a
red carpet for the church that the deacon had purchased without
authority. Poor minister, he was red-headed. He was so mortified
that he resigned and the little church went into a period of inani-
tion. Sometime later the present First Congregational Church was
organized and the firster one gave it the church property plus the
debt for the red carpet. And I think the debt still existed when I
began attending that Sunday School several years later. It was
during the interval of non-activity that the Wilmington church

was organized and the Cerritos people wended their way thither on Sundays until the Methodist church in Compton, much nearer home, was organized.

The road to Wilmington from the Cerritos Ranch went southwest over the mesa and down across bottom lands where corn grew amazingly, so tall that a man could stand on the seat of the spring wagon and not be able to see over the tops of the waving stalks.

And Long Beach? There was none. Where it now stands was a grain field and its only buildings were a shed for horses during threshing times, and the small house occupied during the grain season by Archibald Borden and his four sons from Downey who raised wheat and barley on shares. After the harvest the Bixby sheep were turned in upon the stubble fields.

People were coming into Southern California more and more, especially after rail connection with San Francisco came in 1877. The chorus of rapturous praise singers was swelling, and enterprising people began plotting new settlements. The time for the subdividing of the large holdings came on apace.

I tramped over the level lands on the north end of the ranch, trailing the surveyors who were marking off the acres that were going to the making of Clearwater, and saw it severed from the ranch without a pang, but when Harry and I learned about Mr. Willmore and the American Colony, who wanted Cerritos (Signal) Hill and the bluff and our beach we resented it greatly. There was a seaside town at Santa Monica, — what need of disturbing things as they were for the sake of another? Why should conditions that we had always known, that were as much a part of living as day and night be rudely changed? But the grief of a little boy and little girl could not stay the march of the world and soon we were insulted by fences and gates where before we had ridden unchecked. It wasn't so very long, however, before we became resigned to the town that had first called itself Willmore City and then Long Beach, though we did think it might have kept its own old name, Cerritos Beach. We liked the new hotel bath house which made dressing for a swim much easier than when we had had to run far down the beach to find a projection of bluff large enough to provide modest shelter. And we didn't mind the Methodist Tabernacle with its summer Chautauqua, or the little shop where we could buy fruit, for we seemed to be getting over being children almost as fast as the new town was growing.

But whatever changes have come there has always been the sky,

sunny or starry, or hidden by fog or passing cloud; the same mountains with their wonder of changing color guarded the valley. The
old carpet of gorgeous wild flowers is gone; cities creep over the
plain and a network of roads covers the earth; there is scarcely a
place where one cannot see against the sky the fretted tower that
means oil. One beauty goes and perhaps another comes for those
who have eyes to see, — especially if they have a fair sized blind
spot, which I find sometimes is a most satisfying possession.

The "old timers" wore just as powerful magnifying glasses when
they looked at the future as do certain boosters today. They saw the
possibilities of the development of this Southern California and
prophesied in the face of vacant fields and an unprotected harbor
all the things that have come to pass, and more. It would be pleasant
to know that Heaven afforded peep-holes in its walls through
which these dreamers might look down to see what is now happen-
ing to their adored "land of sunshine." I am sure that Admiral
Henry Knox Thatcher, who commanded the Pacific Squadron from
1866 to 1868, says "I told you so," to grandfather when they meet
on some golden street corner. Wouldn't you, if you had written
this letter to him in the old days on earth?

Nahant, Mass.
Sept. 25th, 1879

My dear friend Hathaway,

. . . .
. . . . During my various visits to the port of San
Pedro I observed the facility with which that Bay could be made a
perfectly secure harbor for ships in all weather by simply building
a mole of stone with wh. the shore is lined for miles. And then
blasting "Dead Man's Island" close at hand for the foundation of
said mole and using the millions of tons of smaller rocks to be found
all along shore for the filling in. At present the anchorage of S. P.
is perfectly safe so long as the wind remains north, — but when
from the south no ship could escape destruction at that anchorage
unless supplied with steam power. I foresaw that San Francisco
would strongly oppose any attempt to make S. P. a port of entry
because it would deprive them of the power of plundering that fair
and fertile portion of California as they now do. And all the products of that (best) portion of the state must now be carried at great
cost to the only exporting custom house, S. F., whereas if they could
be shipped directly from S. P. the producers would save tens of
thousands annually even now. But now is as nothing, for the day is

not far distant when Los Angeles and adjoining counties will become the greatest producing counties on the face of the globe; everything points to it, a soil of unsurpassed fertility, and a climate as perfect as is to be found upon earth. It is but for the people themselves to wake up and *insist* upon aid from government in accomplishing this noble work. With my feeble efforts I did what I could to bring this about during my command of the Pacific Squadron and secured the aid of the Republican member of Congress from C. to induce Govm't. to send out an able engineer to survey the Port of S. P. with this object in view. I wrote articles for the S. F. newspapers and had hopes of success but my term of command expired and my successor felt no interest in the matter and the few producers at that time appeared quite indifferent except Mr. Banning of Wilmington, who seemed to be a man of enlarged views and was then in public life and exerting considerable influence. But I think the S. F. element was too strong for him to contend with. Yet I am satisfied that this scheme will one day be accomplished, though I may not live to see it. I felt at the time not a little sorry that friend Jotham (who was as deeply interested as any) did not take more thought on the subject of building up that lovely country; of course the R. R. will aid in developing that lower section of California but it will be found a very expensive mode of transportation compared with the floating process. These are all crude ideas of mine you will say perhaps, but they have taken firm possession of my mind and will hardly be eradicated.

.   .   .   .

Affectionate friend, H. K. Thatcher.

Admiral Thatcher was the grandson of Gen. Henry Knox, Washington's first Secretary of War.

It is interesting to note that the prediction that the country about Los Angeles would become the greatest producing county in the world has been fulfilled so far as the United States is concerned, for in the 1920 census it is ranked first in agricultural production. Before the time of the writing of the letter work was begun and a considerable break-water built, following in general the lines suggested. The present development of San Pedro Harbor, now generally called Los Angeles Harbor, reads like a fairy story.

CHAPTER XIII

School Days

My education began the day I was born, for I am told that, after a somewhat precipitous and unceremonious arrival, my father took me about the room to see the pictures on the wall — sundry chromos and steel engravings, which I am said to have observed with intelligence and pleasure. Having been intimately acquainted with several normal infants, I doubt, however, both observation and pleasure. Perhaps that early exposure to art was what determined my life-long interest in it, and in the joys of seeing. Those old-fashioned pictures may have presented to my inexperienced eye no more confused an image than do the latest post-impressionist interpretations of essential form or the soul of things to my trained sight.

After this introduction to the graphic arts I met poetry — familiar hymns and Mother Goose. I knew the ten little Indians who by a series of gruesome accidents were reduced to none, Prudy, Sanford and Merton whom I loathed, Pocahontas and Robinson Crusoe. I still possess a number of books that date far back in my life, among them Mary Mapes Dodge's *Rhymes and Jingles* and Whittier's *Child Life*. The only things my father ever read aloud to me were poems, usually out of the big green and gold *Household Book of Poetry*. Aunt Martha read us *Helen's Babies*, to my delight.

I was reading at four. I have "Rewards of Merit," small cards with gay pictures given me at the end of each week when I had been a good little girl and made proper progress in my reading lessons. And for my fifth birthday my father printed in red ink a foolscap sheet of words for me to learn to spell, five columns beginning with words of two letters and running up to six letters each. I must have been greatly pleased with my present for I remember it yet so happily. A letter written by my mother at this time says that I was insatiable in my demand for stories to be told to me and for books to be read.

I went to a school for the first time just after I was seven. It was a private one located on the north side of First Street between Spring and Main in Los Angeles. I remember very little about it. My career there was ended by the long sickness when father told me about his early trips to California. The next school was supposed to be very select, Miss Carle's, over on Olive Street near Second in the same house with Miss Stem, my Adventist music teacher, who used to tell me the world was about to end, but who could give no satisfactory answer to my contention that in that case I ought to be having harp lessons instead of piano. The school numbered ten children and was conducted in Miss Carle's bedroom, apparently, for in one corner stood a marvelous high feather-bed; once when I carelessly stood on a chair to reach the top of the black-board, she in anger tossed me across the room to this bed, where I disappeared in its feathery depths. Having acquired a little knowledge and considerable whooping-cough, this school was also consigned to my past.

The Los Angeles Academy on Main Street, between Third and Fourth, was my next educational resort. This was on the lot adjoining the famous old round-house, or better, fourteen-sided house. Over each window of the second story was painted a name of a state, one California, the others the names of the original thirteen colonies. It had been for many years a popular resort and beer garden called "The Garden of Eden." But its days of glory were past, and the marble Adam and Eve who had adorned it were gone; no flaming sword was visible, but there was a formidable cactus hedge on the Spring Street side which may have deterred them from return. There was vacant land on the east side of Main Street opposite the school, where one of the city zanjas ran beside a row of willows at the foot of a little hill. Playing here one noon I attempted to wade and was unceremoniously swept from my feet and sent sailing down the flume. I suppose I learned something at this school, but I know that I have always suffered from lack of drill in plain addition and subtraction, so I think I shall have to blame the Los Angeles Academy for hampering me in calculus and other of the higher reaches of mathematics.

When I was ten I was somewhat desperately and gingerly consigned to the public schools, where I would much better have been from the beginning. I started in the fifth grade under Mrs. Ella Enderlein, later a newspaper woman well known in the city. I had the good fortune to have both sixth and seventh grade work with Mrs. C. G. Du Bois, a rare teacher, who remained in the school system for many, many years, and will be lovingly remembered by numerous men and women of Los Angeles who were also once the boys and girls of this city. When I knew her she wore six little grey curls hanging at the back of her head, and she had the merriest blue eyes, — we learned our lessons well for her. There was a strange principal who used to walk about the halls arrayed like Solomon in all his glory. He wore slippers and a dressing gown of oriental pattern and coloring, trimmed with a sapphire blue. Perhaps this style of dress had something to do with his disappearance from our view. His successor was an excellent teacher, I know, for he taught me in the eighth grade; however he had a bad temper and once threw an eraser at one of the girls and chased a boy up and down the aisles and over our desks in a vain attempt to thrash him.

Mrs. Bradfield was art teacher for all the schools in the city and gave me my first lessons. As I had something of a gift for drawing I was allowed on all possible public occasions to decorate the black-boards with colored chalk pictures and designs, often Kate Green-away children, or sun-flowers after Oscar Wilde.

My four years of grammar school were passed in the first high school building, located on Pound Cake Hill, about where the upper story of the County Court House now is. When the site was wanted by the men folk of the town, the school building was moved on a mighty trestle across Temple Street and over to California Street and the hill itself was decapitated.

When I was ready for high school I went down to the new gram-mar school building at Sixth Street which occupied the Mercantile Place property between Spring and Broadway. I daily walked along a Broadway of cottages and gardens and occasional churches. Often I picked a flower or a Chinese orange from Aunt Margaret's yard at Second Street; and, as I passed, I looked down the lovely Third Street, shaded by large pepper trees, to a cottage covered by an enormous rose bush.

The Los Angeles High School was temporarily accommodated in four rooms and an office, while the new building up next the old graveyard on North Hill Street, was being constructed. It is said that for several years the high school children ate their noon lunches sitting on tombs and cemetery curbs. In my day there were fewer than two hundred students. The course was not unlike the simpler ones of to-day, but there were not so many electives and none of the manual and technical classes. In the ninth grade I had

Latin, Rhetoric, Algebra, Phyiscal Geography, and Ancient History; and in the tenth, Latin, Geometry, English and English History, — not so very different from the present college preparatory, is it?

Mrs. Bradfield taught drawing in the high school as well as in the grades. It was under her that Guy Rose got his first art lessons. Music also had a special teacher and under Prof. Kent we sang lustily — among other things *We are the gay students of fair Salamanca.* His high silk hat, his close fitting Prince Albert coat, his waxed moustache, his smile, and tripping steps were very entertaining to the children.

At this time it was determined to send me north to school for a change of climate. Oakland at that time was a center of private schools and academies. I went to Field Seminary, long since extinct. The life in a well-governed boarding school was something new to me. I, who had ranged freely, must take my daily exercise in a regulated walk, the girls going two by two up and down the city streets. It was surprising how soon this habit affected my point of view. Once, after due deliberation and considering of my record, recommendations, and pedigree, I was allowed to walk alone around the corner — no street was to be crossed — to take dinner with my cousins, the Ben Flint family. It is a wonder I did not crawl through the paling fence where the back yards met, for such was the effect of the constant mass movements that when I stepped alone out of the gate into the peaceful street I felt as embarrassed as if I had shed my garments, along with the protecting phalanx of pupils and guarding teacher.

On Thursdays I was excused from exercise to take a bath. The rule of the clock was rigid, and when it said four o'clock on Thursday I must be ready to enter and bathe, or go forever unbathed. What a smashing of precedent! But I suppose one tub could not accommodate over forty girls on Saturday night, the correct American bath night.

The actual school work was a delight, with glimpses into new fields: chemistry, where we saw samples of aluminum, a metal which might some day become very useful; geology, with a long trip on the street car miles and miles into the country to the State University at Berkeley, where Professor Le Conte told us most interesting things — geology, gently tuned by Professor Thomas Heaton to meet the exigencies of Mosaic "days of creation," and yet opening the mind to questionings. There was also Cicero and an introduction into the German language and English literature. I even read the whole of *Paradise Lost*. Then, bad eyes, and a verdict of never any more school, not even sight enough for sewing! But oculists don't know everything always.

And so I came home. In the house were many books, — always had been so long as I could remember. The rigid Maine rule of semi-annual house-cleaning held sway, and it was often my task to take out, beat, dust and replace all the volumes in the capacious bookcases. There were essays, histories, biographies: sets of Dickens, Thackeray, George Eliot, Hawthorne, Scott, besides scattered novels; Shakespeare was there and a few other dramatists, all the standard poets, Cervantes and Plutarch. These were not only dusted, but read to a great extent.

Harper's Magazine, with its buff cover adorned with cupids, cornucopias, fruits and flowers, was a regular visitor, as was the *Century* later. I recall the laughter of a family reading of Frank Stockton's *The Casting Away of Mrs. Lecks and Mrs. Aleshine*. *The Congregationalist* and *The Pacific* provided Sunday reading for father, along with his Bagster's *Bible*. He once pointed out to me mildly that the varying accounts of the Hebrew historical events did not "jibe." Several missionary magazines gave knowledge of life in far parts of the world. *Littell's Living Age* came for several years, and, being bound, was at least handled semi-annually.

The tri-weekly *New York Tribune* and *Harper's Weekly* (until it turned mug wump) brought news out of the East to supplement what two daily papers afforded. I think father knew where every raw material in the world was produced and where it was manufactured. He used to "poke fun" at me as an educated woman, after I returned from college, because I could not name, characterize and assign to his state every United States Senator.

I had the advantage of a home where good English was spoken, where one was expected to know how to spell correctly and write grammatically, where an interest was taken in large and wide questions, and where everyone found his chief pleasure and amusement in reading. Rather a bad environment in which to find oneself condemned to useless eyes!

Los Angeles did not in those day offer, naturally, the same opportunities in art, theater, and music that the East did, but I saw Booth and Barrett in *Julius Caesar* and I heard Adelina Patti.

When Aunt Martha came to us, she brought with her a hundred photographic copies of the world's famous paintings and pictures of cathedrals and statuary. On many a Sunday afternoon I pored over these until the names of Raphael, da Vinci, Murillo, Phidias became as familiar as Longfellow or Scott.

As was customary, a faithful attempt extending over many years, was made to make a musician out of me. It failed. I was eye-minded. That exposure to art on my natal day had determined my tastes.

Vacations, the most welcome part of the school year, were spent, with the exception of one summer in the East, for the most part at the Cerritos. As the resort grew at Long Beach and we young folks attained age we passed many hours on the sand and in the breakers.

I hold memories of horseback rides at night on the broad strand when the moon made magic on the sea and in the romantic heart of youth.

I had my first experience of camp life at Catalina Island. Avalon was newly established, with the first hotel, a wharf and a store or two. We and our friends, the Dr. Dole family, had tents at the water's edge in the present center of town. The *S. S. Hermosa* was our means of transport from San Pedro and its arrival was the one local excitement. No telephones, no aeroplanes, one or two yachts, possibly a dozen row boats, no roads, no trees or flowers in Avalon, but quiet, joy and informality.

The smooth water of the bay gave me the opportunity for learning to swim which the frequency of great waves at Long Beach had hindered. It was during this happy summer I reached the advanced age of eighteen, and I smile when I recall the solemnity with which I said within my heart goodbye to childhood.

It was on the island that I did my first tramping over long trails in fragrant hills and slept by night rolled in a blanket on the ground. The hiking clothes we women wore would excite derision today. Our modest skirts were wool and of ankle length — fine for threading our way through brush and cactus! However, Sara Dole and Miss Wilson, incipient modernists, boldly and brazenly donned bathing suits to climb mountain tops, — bathing suits whose navy blue flannel skirts reached only an inch or so below the knee, although no similar shortage exposed wrist or elbow.

A little later I climbed both Wilson Peak and Old Baldy, the former afforded camp shelter for the night with a wide fireplace in the common room. It was the period between the first astronomical venture there and the beginning of the present one. In the morning we saw the sun shine on the top of a valley full of white clouds.

A few weeks before this trip I went with a group of the graduates of the first class of Pomona College to the top of Baldy. We had some mules to help, but it must be remembered that there were only rough trails in the mountains, not even a wagon road over Hogsback. And we toiled and boiled and blistered and burned our way to the top. A few of us stayed overnight on the mountain. As the evening fell the thin air chilled. There was snow in sheltered hollows. Just below the bald top we huddled and shivered and fitfully slept close to the fire kept by the gallant boys. In the majesty of the first morning, out over falling ridge and shadowed cañon, out over the gray far desert we watched the Sun God wake.

CHAPTER XIV

Pioneering at Pomona College

"IT must be a college of the New England type — just where and how it is to be started is the question," said one of the men who, one evening in the middle eighties, were discussing with my father and grandfather the possibility and need of a good college in Southern California, one of high standards of character and scholarship. There was no question of necessity — only of ways and means. The boys and girls must be given the same type of education as that offered in the far away homeland.

Southern California was booming, and hearts and hopes were high. It was a bold undertaking for the small group of Congregationalists, but with faith and hard work and time it could be done — the founding of a college, "Christian, not sectarian — for both sexes," a slogan from the first. Later the hopes and dreams of the few crystallized into action and the word came home that a committee had been appointed to find a location.

After much jaunting, even so far as Banning, on the east, the choice fell upon Piedmont, a sightly mesa north of Pomona, a little town that had recently been growing up some forty miles east of Los Angeles; and until a permanent name could be decided upon (possibly that of some devoted donor) the venture was to be named "The Pomona College." This name was not finally accepted for some twenty years.

From time to time I heard of the progress of the undertaking. Father's cousin, Nathan Blanchard, who had been disappointed in his boyhood ambition for a college education in Maine, was much concerned in this project for providing opportunity for the young people of his later state. He became one of the first trustees, and continued on the board and was vitally interested so long as he lived. It was to his generosity that the college owes its beautiful acreage of oaks and native growth, Blanchard Park.

Rev. Charles B. Sumner, the minister of the Pomona Congregational church, had secured a young man, Frank Brackett, recently graduated from Dartmouth, to open a private school in Pomona. It met in the church parlor. Mr. Sumner's son and daughter and a few others needed a chance to prepare for college. After about six months the authorities of the new college took over this school as a preparatory department — teachers, students, and all.

In the meantime, plans for a permanent building were maturing, and amid hopes and prayers, joy and a certain trepidation, the corner stone was laid on the beautiful heights at the mouth of Live Oak Cañon, close to the mountain, with a wide outlook over the valley.

When plans for the college first took form, Southern California was full of hope and enthusiasm — those were the boom days. Men were making fortunes over night, and the generosity of many hearts promised sufficient support for the college. But the point of saturation in land speculation was reached and a panic was precipitated and the new-born enterprise faced disaster. Then began years of self-denial, struggle, devotion, visions that have resulted in the college known today. Many a time it was a very serious question whether or not the breath of life could be kept in the baby.

About the time I came home from Field Seminary, condemned to no more school, the young institution was offered the empty hotel in the unsuccessful boom town of Claremont, together with certain lots staked out about it. The trustees decided to accept the gift, planning to use this site ultimately for the preparatory work only, and to go on with its college buildings at Piedmont as originally intended.

The following June the school introduced itself with closing exercises, oral examinations, etc. Grandfather was among the guests. Although he was now over eighty, he spent much of every day with books, reading constantly his Greek or Latin, or solving mathematical problems for sheer joy in it. He was delighted by an oral examination in Greek given by a Mr. Norton, the new head of the school. One boy especially pleased him by showing evidence of good teaching and by the gusto with which he translated his Homer. He "believed the boy was the son of Deacon Barrows of the Ojai." Perhaps this same boy's enthusiasm for the war exploits of Homer is responsible for the military fervor of the man.

So when I decided that my eyes, fortified by glasses, were not yet gone, and that I must go to school again, grandfather suggested that I try the new one at Pomona. "Of course it is pioneering, but seems genuine and worth trying," he said. Consequently, on a hot August day, Aunt Martha and I went forth to investigate, and, perhaps beginning a long line of the mistaken, sought Pomona College in Pomona.

After some delay we found a man with an express wagon who took us to Claremont, an hour's drive under a scorching noonday sun. We soon left the little settlement, passed the apricot and peach orchards that have since been replaced by oranges, and struck off in a diagonal through virgin land to the large building, gabled and turreted, standing alone in the distance. As we came nearer we discovered that there was more town than we had realized. The same Santa Fe station that is now in use was in its place — would that we had arrived there instead of at the Southern Pacific in Pomona!

On the sandy road, now Yale Avenue, there was one store, which contained the post-office, — a primitive department store kept by Mr. Urbanus, whose name was the only suggestion of a city in the region. A little farther up the road was a spare white box of a house, which has since grown porches and a garden, where we found the principal of the school, Mr. Norton, with his wife and baby girl, Catharine. To the east was Mr. Biely's barn; to the west Colonel W. H. Holabird's two-storied house; and two or three other small empty houses peeked over the top of the brush. On the outskirts rose an imposing red and yellow towered and ornamented schoolhouse, waiting for the children of the visioned city to materialize. Some twenty years later it was supplanted by the present attractive grammar school, moved across the street, and, with form and color made more modest, given over to the use of the city fathers.

The ex-hotel belonged to the same architectural period as the Del Monte at Monterey or the Coronado at San Diego, but naturally it was of lesser glory.

Such was Claremont in 1889; no streets, no walks, just a few spots reclaimed from the desert, connected by trails or sandy roads; all the rest sage, cactus, stones, an occasional oak or sycamore; but the same ever-beautiful and mysterious mountains stood guard, the same sunny skies and fragrant air gave charm. Rabbits scuttled between the bushes, lizards and horned toads enjoyed the climate, rattlesnakes found a peaceful home, and at night coyotes ranged and sang.

A little clearing had been made about the aforetime hotel now devoted to the incipient college, and vines and trees had been planted but as yet they had not made sufficient growth to be noticeable. The oak tree that now stands in the center of College Avenue was then in its native state in the midst of the brush. The building with its meager furnishing had stood empty all summer and accumulated dust added to its dreariness. However the plan of work offered me was attractive and, much to the surprise of my aunt, I decided to enter in the fall, thus beginning the procession of children, grandchildren, great-grandchildren of the old scholar who from that day to this have been connected with the college.

In September the third member of the so-called "old faculty," Miss Spalding, arrived. She was destined to develop the English department, but this year filled in, teaching Latin, German, spelling and composition, and how many other subjects I do not know.

All the activities of the school were in the one building. The large parlor with the circular window was chapel and assembly room. The room occupied in recent years by the Dean of Women was study hall for the younger students; Prof. Norton had a small class-room on the east side, Miss Spalding had half the dining room roughly partitioned off, and Prof. Brackett dispensed mathematics and physics over the bar in the hotel bar-room. He dispensed the physics so successfully that I was able three years later in Wellesley College to rely once or twice on Claremont knowledge to carry me through a physics lesson otherwise unprepared.

The Hall housed all the resident members of the school except Mr. Norton's family. Mr. Brackett and his bride were on the first floor; and upstairs, divided by a partition, pervious to sounds and notes, if not to persons, were the men's and women's dormitories — eleven boys in the former, four girls and two teachers in the latter. Here also roomed Miss Roe, sister of E. P. Roe of *Chestnut Burr* fame, a forerunner of the easterners who now make Claremont their winter home.

At this time there were about sixty students in the school, only one of them, Helen Sumner, being of college rank. In the senior preparatory class which I joined, there were about a dozen. They formed the unique class that for seven years was the most advanced in the school — think how dangerous to heads the experience of being seniors for seven years! This class graduated from Pomona college in 1894 and numbered among its members Dr. George Sumner and Dr. David P. Barrows.

The year I joined them I found each member of the class had read Caesar during the summer vacation, taking examination and passing in September in order that the class might go on with the required amount of Cicero in the first semester and Vergil in the second, and so make college the next fall, with four years of Latin done, and done thoroughly in two years. With Vergil at nine in the morning (after submitting to ten minutes of spelling drill on any word Miss Spaulding might find in Dr. Johnson's *Rasselas*), and again at four in the afternoon we read rapidly enough to get the charm of the poem as well as the dry bones of vocabulary and construction. All the work of the year was strenuous but full of delight — the happiest year of all my school life.

The primitive conditions of a pioneer school only added zest to the students, but for those teachers who had come out of the East the barn-like hotel in the desert, the lack of comforts and conveniences, even of sufficient food, and the meager salaries possible meant hardship.

One of the institutions of our day was the bus which met students from Pomona who came to North Pomona on the "dummy," which I recognized as the discarded, first means of transportation between Long Beach and the outside world. Down there it had been known as the G. O. P., "Get Out and Push," because frequently the male passengers had to dismount and help propel it when it hesitated in its progress from Thenard, the junction on the main S. P. line near Wilmington, to the little camp-meeting settlement on the bluff, Long Beach. When it was superseded there it evidently had been transferred to the remote service between Pomona and the new Santa Fe Railroad to the north of the town.

The bus was very rickety, two long seats whose cushions sprouted excelsior, a somewhat tremulous canopy top, a rear step that swung loose so that it required great skill to mount, especially since there was a hole in the floor where one would naturally place one's foot in entering. It must have been a gift bus, into whose mouth one must not look enquiringly.

Bret Harte, a high, bony, bay horse, and Amos Obediah Jonah Micah, a roly-poly squat sorrel were the mis-mated pair who provided locomotion. I was once told that the bones of one of these horses is preserved in the college museum, but an after thought on the part of the informer, suggested that the historic skeleton might have upheld one of the steeds celebrated a year or two later, — Bismarck or Gladstone or Mephistopheles. Speaking of the latter reminds me of a story once current in Claremont concerning a conversation between the heads of the Latin and Greek departments. "I can make a pun on any word you will propose," said Professor

Colcord. "How about the name of my horse?" replied Professor Norton. Quick as a wink came the response, "If I had him here I could hit him with me-fist-awful-easy."

My year in Claremont was an unusually rainy one, and for a time all the lower part of town was under water from outbreaking springs. It was welcomed by John McCall, the boy who drove the bus, as a providential means of extending the usefulness of the public conveyance. Every night he took the bus to the point now called the corner of Second Street and Alexander Avenue, un-hitched Bret and Amos, and left it standing in the water all night, so that the rims of the wheels might swell enough to retain the tires the next day.

On Sundays the bus must forego its day of rest in order to take Claremont to Pomona to church, the former town not yet having a church of its own. We enlivened the long, slow drive home, more than an hour in our slow-going chariot, with calling up memories of all the good things to eat we had ever known or imagined. We were none too well fed at best and Sunday dinner came late. It is certain that we did not suffer from over-feeding, but, on the other hand, I suppose our minds were all the clearer for our restrained diet.

This was the time of the beginning of things. The Pomona College Literary Society — high sounding name — had begun its career. Debates, papers, three-minute ex-tempore speeches were taken seriously. One gala day in spring we turned to Mother Goose and treated her works in the same manner in which we had been handling Shakespeare. One number on the program was a debate on "Was the mother justified in whipping Jill on the occasion when she and Jack went for water?" I remember it well for I defended Jill in opposition to David Barrows. It was the first time that either of us had delivered a speech without notes. Unfortunately, I lost — but who could expect to win against the eloquence and, I maintained at the time, the sophistry of an embryo University President? However, it was a split verdict and one of the judges resisted his plausible arguments and gave credit to the weight of my feminine defense of poor Jill. (Thank you, Dr. C. B. Sumner!) The debate was great fun.

This year the college paper was born, and christened the *Pomona Student*. It was a monthly, and, considering that it was conducted by preparatory students, compares very well with its later representative, even if I, who was its maid-of-all-work, do say so.

There was a music department, with Miss Stella Fitch as teacher. During the next few years music became quite a feature, and its quality is recalled with pleasure and regret in these days of prevailing jazz.

As for athletics, tennis and baseball had arrived, but no football or track work. Several students had their own saddle horses and one or two could be hired. A happy memory is of a spring day, a ride through the fragrant sagebrush, a running race down Ontario's long street, — a good time even if I did wear a long black habit and ride a sidesaddle.

On the first Mountain Day we went to Live Oak Cañon — perhaps thirty of us. We led the outdoor life that has always been so large a part of Pomona College attractiveness. I wonder if any one since my day, after a picnic in the Wash, enjoyed an afternoon of sledding. Four of us, naturally two boys and two girls, once topped off a "steak-feed" by sliding down the short, grassy slope of the knoll, south of the present Greek Theatre, with a frying pan and an iron baker for our sleds.

The heating arrangements in the Hall were primitive, so that a minor object of every walk was to collect combustible material. I'm afraid that a good many corner lot stakes went up in our smoke. The little stoves were amusing. As I remember them, they seem about six inches square, by twelve long, but I suppose they really must have been at least ten by fifteen. One day I went in under the Hall in search of chips left from the building, but meeting there two cunning little black and white wood pussies, I quickly and silently retreated, lest they should consider me a poacher on their preserves and protest.

The college library at that time occupied partially half a dozen shelves in an alcove. Miss Spalding, who had brought two hundred books with her out of the East as a nucleus for the library was in charge, and in the spring term inspired us to see how much we could earn for its benefit. Soon all sorts of enterprises were under way. Our dining table instituted a system of penny fines for tardiness or slang. I was book-keeper and still hold the record. Individuals offered their wares or talents for the fund. In the April number of the *Student* I find various advertisements: "We sadly look at our tattered garments, but suddenly our faces light up, for we remember that Miss Metkiff darns at 1 cent per square inch." "R. S. Day, Jr., famous tonsorial artist. Hair cut, fifteen cents; shave, ten cents. Bangs cut and curled, ten cents; long hair shampooed twenty-five

cents; short hair, ten cents." Attractive rates offered by the first
Claremont barber, you must admit.

I, who owned one of the original kodaks, taking pictures about
the size of a butter plate, made one very successful photograph.
Rev. E. S. Williams, a visitor at the college, volunteered to give
Bancroft's *History of the United States* to the infant library in
exchange for a picture of the Student Body. Our labors netted much
fun, the history, and about thirty dollars.

Excitement grew as Commencement approached, for a class of
eleven was ready for college and in September the actual work of
college grade would begin. Although the closing exercises were
made much of, and guests came from all over Southern California,
we youngsters were never allowed to forget that we were merely
"preps," and, lest we should imagine ourselves of too much importance, no diplomas were allowed us. We were told by Mr. Norton that we were "nothing but kids." To remedy this lack of evidence of our graduation, two of us picked out, finger by finger, on
the only typewriter in town, diplomas modeled on an Amherst one,
in which we granted ourselves the degree of "Haedi (kids) in
Artibus." These we distributed at our class supper, served in Mr.
Brackett's bar room. On this occasion our class prophet established
her claim to be a seer for she said, speaking of David Barrows:

"What are you, priest, poet or philosopher?"

"I am in the P's at any rate, — purveyor."

"Of mental merchandise," said his sister.

"Allow me," said a merry voice at my elbow, "to introduce Mr.
Barrows, H.A., B.A., M.A., D.D., LL.D., Ph.D., president of
. . . . college, the leader of young shoots in the way they
should go."

Perhaps Vere Metkiff was a suggestor rather than a seer, and it
may have been this prophecy that set the boy in the path to the presidency of the University of California. I observe, however, that he
is still minus the proposed degree of D.D.

The next day a boy and girl sat all day on the stairs of Claremont
Hall and crammed Roman History out of two brick-red primers,
and in the afternoon took two college entrance examinations, to
meet necessary requirements. And they both passed. And perhaps
they know as much Roman History now as if they had spent months
instead of hours in its study.

And so the year ended, and I left to go east to college as had
been planned for me so long as I could remember. But had there

not been stiffer backbones than mine at home, I think I would have been a member of that first class at Pomona.

My friends did not forget me, and twice I hurried home from Wellesley to go into camp with them up in San Antonio Cañon, two wonderful experiences. Our party of twenty-six was the first of any size to go beyond Hogsback. We had to go to its base by wagon, and then over the trail, walking on up to the mouth of Bear Cañon where we stayed for ten days. From here a dozen of us made the ascent of the peak which I have described.

The three teachers, Prof. Brackett, Dr. Norton, and Dr. Spalding, whom I knew in that long ago day of the beginning of things, have all these years been giving of their strength and knowledge. And Dr. C. B. Sumner, who dreamed and planned and worked for the college, lives to see it established and prosper, its bare, single building grown to the beautiful campus and many buildings of the present, its student body increased more than tenfold, while his son, the youngest of that famous class, has for years been a valued and loved professor in the strong and growing college of today.

CHAPTER XV

Conclusion

T H E first shovelful of earth was turned for Wellesley College the day before I was born, and when I was ready to enter as a student, only eleven classes had been graduated. Yet to me, coming as I did, from the embryonic, frontier college, with its single building in a waste of cactus and sagebrush, Wellesley, with its many dignified buildings set beside Lake Waban in a campus of sweeping lawns and stately trees, seemed an institution not only honorable, but ancient. Because of my three earlier visits in the East, the conditions of climate and of village life were not unknown to me, but it was the four continuous college years spent in the environment to which my race was wont, and to which my instinct responded, that brought me my heritage of joy in the slipping seasons, and made possible an understanding reading of the songs of our English tongue from *Sumer is icumen in* to *When lilacs last in the dooryard bloomed.*

Wellesley's hills and meadows, her trees, her birds, her lake brought me an ecstasy that lingers; her out-of-doors became an integral part of me, stored pictures of the wide whiteness of winter, with snow-laden firs or interlacing crystal branches, or of an autumn sunset sky, glorious behind a black screen of naked trees; memories of hepaticas and snowdrops in early spring, of anemones and crowfoot violets; of a mist of new pale leaves on the elms and red buds on the maples; of lushness of green June, and waxen lilies on summer streams, a greenness and wetness unlike my land at home, unlike my California with its wide skies and open miles, its great mountains, its grays and tans, its far blues and wistful purples. It is blessed I am to know two homes.

Time in its passing brought me to college, not the one to which I had been destined from birth, Mt. Holyoke, but to Wellesley. The former had not then transformed itself from a female seminary into a woman's college, so, since the value of a degree for women had become increasingly apparent, it was deemed wise for the girl going three thousand miles to school to go to the institution of the higher rank. Neither Berkeley nor Stanford University, though near home, had been considered. The State University was of necessity non-religious and hence somewhat suspect of the orthodox, and Stanford was new and untried — and besides — didn't it derive its support from race horses and a winery? Moreover, New England parentage and tradition sent the children "home," if possible, for their education.

With Mt. Holyoke eliminated, the choice lay between Smith and Wellesley, and fell upon the latter for the following reasons:

In the first place, Wellesley was reputed to be modeled on the beloved school of Mary Lyon, and to have preserved some of its best features. In the second place — the location near Boston gave it an advantage over its sister inland college in the way of music, art, libraries, museums. It was also, by virtue of its situation, more accessible to visitors, and many a notable person, drawn by the glamour that still lingered about a woman's college, came to inspect the materialization of Tennyson's vision of *The Princess.* The inspection of visitors and girls was mutual, and, we hope, of advantage to both. In the third place, and this is what finally decided me, I preferred the course of study.

I entered college on certificate, covering the work I had done in three schools, the Los Angeles High School, Field Seminary in Oakland, and Pomona College Preparatory School in Claremont. So far as I can judge, my western preparation was as effective as that of my classmates who came from the East and the Middle West.

College life is broken by vacations. I was fortunate in being able to return to my home for the long summers, while seeing various parts of the East during the shorter recesses. With great delight each June I left Massachusetts, beautiful to look upon, intolerable to live in, going to California's comfortable southwest coast. I was always sped on my way by the pities of my friends who ignorantly supposed that California climate is as much warmer than the eastern in summer as it is in winter. I doubt if any of my friends were so cool as I.

The eight trips back and forth across the continent gave opportunity to see many different places. One journey by the Canadian Pacific gave glimpses of the old city of Montreal, of the lovely land north of Lake Superior and of the grandeur of the great northern Rockies. On another trip a stop-over in Chicago gave me ten days at the Columbian Exposition, whose chief memory is of the dignified white buildings, the art collection, and the lighted lagoons at night.

My shorter vacations included one each in Chicago, Boston, New York City, and Washington, where I had the privilege of seeing how actual sessions of Congress compared with our college representations. I discovered that we at college had neglected some of the stage furniture — the couches upon which exhausted congressmen took their daily siesta.

Twice I spent Christmas in Skowhegan, Maine, my mother's old home town to which she had taken me in my little girl days. Here I found deep snows and a temperature forty degrees below, and in my hostess the truest embodiment of the Christmas spirit I have ever met.

A Christmas vacation spent in Boston was one of the most interesting. A friend and I took a room high up in an old house near Copley Square — two girls free to enjoy the city. Among other delights we had a feast of music — the Haydn and Handel Society *Messiah*, a recital given by Paderewski, the new Polish pianist, two symphony concerts, heard from the twenty-five cent gallery of the old Symphony Hall, the Christmas music at the Church of the Ascension, and the memorable watch-night service, New Year's Eve, at Trinity Church, when everyone hoped and no one knew that Phillips Brooks would come. The church was dim and fragrant with the odor of cedar and pine, and the people were hushed by the beauty of the ancient ritual. As midnight approached the great figure of the bishop appeared from among the trees of the choir and mounted the pulpit. Bishop Brooks spoke simply and solemnly and as the hour struck made a prayer out of his own deep heart. With his message for the New Year we went into an unforgettable, marvellous night, with snowy ground, a dark sky filled with fleecy clouds about a prismed moon. In three weeks the beloved Bishop was dead — a true bishop of all the people. The knowing of Phillips Brooks was one of the good things my years in Wellesley brought me.

College days were over. I was a graduate of Wellesley, with all that meant of training, of prestige, of obligation.

The four years had been busy and valuable, but they were not the happiest days of my life, as school days are often said to be. I was going through a period of re-adjustment and re-valuation that did not make for peace of mind. I was often lonely, for, although I had a wide and pleasant acquaintance, I did not make the intimate

friends that I did either before or after college days. I have wondered why. Was I so unsettled that no one *me* dominated and
attracted its own, or was I, the western girl, always something of a
stranger in a strange land? It may have been better so, since I was
to go so far from college haunts and friends. The girls at the end
sang pensively of Seniors about to be "lost in the wide, wide world."
I didn't care or fear. I hastened to be lost, for the wide, wide world
meant California, my homeland, to which I fled the instant I secured my diploma. The western girl who went East to college went
West to live.

The years at Wellesley soon slipped back into the dim region of
memory and Los Angeles became once more the familiar environment of my life. It was so good to be at home again — but Time
was bringing changes and new repsonsibilities. The family was
smaller than it had been, for my sister had followed me to Wellesley, and my aunt was taking a year-long vacation in the East,
thus giving me a chance to learn by experience how to be a house-
keeper. I judge that I, the amateur, did not always reach the usual
standard of good order set for our home, for I have a picture of
my father down on his knees at the parlor fireplace, one evening
before dinner when company was expected, carefully wiping the
blower with an oiled rag, while suggesting to me "I think if your
Aunt Marthy were here she would take those newspapers from the
shelf under the table." I did not know that he noticed such things.
I was a bit conscience-smitten.

Our life went on serenely and happily. Daily he went down the
hill to the company office on First Street, just above Broadway. We
filled our home time with reading the newspapers, books and magazines, especially *The Forum*, which at that time was very good. I
made a final fruitless attempt to be musical, took a few painting
lessons which I wish had been many, and for a time went to the new
Throop Institute in Pasadena, for dressmaking training. I learned
how to bone a basque and line a skirt, and a few other arts now
unnecessary.

On Sunday I undertook to hold the attention of half a dozen
lively small boys. We liked each other and had a very good time
together, but how much we learned I cannot say. Perhaps my own
sons have profited by my acquaintance with those other obstrep-
erous young Americans. I never wanted to exchange them for the
neighboring class of little girls whose whispers and giggles were
less understandable to me than the excess of energy evidenced by
punching, pin-sticking, and the tipping over of chairs.

Neither father nor I was very demonstrative, but we enjoyed being together as we always had. We went out seldom in the evening as a growing deafness made public meetings of little value to him. But we never missed a Maine Society gathering. He had not lost his interest in people from the old home state and read the *Great Register* whenever it came out, checking off every "Mainiac" and hunting him up when possible.

One evening when a cousin, Frank Weston from Santa Clara, was visiting us I heard him and father exchanging news of one and another relative unknown to me, so I asked how many cousins there were; they did not know; but father began naming them for me to count. He remembered one hundred and twenty-five, no seconds being listed. How many firsts he may have missed, I do not know. They all seemed to know him and whenever a new one came to California he made for our house. There was a certain quality about father that won people. I remember the testimony to this that I witnessed about this time when he and I had gone to a church supper together. He soon saw a strange, small baby whom he borrowed and carried about with him all evening, to the apparent satisfaction of both. It is a pity that his children came so late in life that he had no chance to be grandfather to the fifteen grandchildren that have accrued since his death.

The spring of 1896 brought a sudden dismay into our peaceful family. A telegram from New York City reported the desperate illness of Nan, who had gone there for her Easter vacation. Aunt Martha hurried to her, while we at home for six weeks lived for the daily telegram. The anxiety told on father, who was then past seventy. Even after my sister's safe return he still seemed weary.

That was the summer of the Free Silver campaign, and he was greatly worried about the outcome and its effect upon his somewhat precarious business affairs. Even his satisfaction at the defeat of Mr. Bryan was offset by the strain of an all-night session counting ballots in a cold polling place, he having been unable to resist the temptation to accept his customary position as an election officer of his precinct. With McKinley elected and Nan well the world was saved!

And then, early in December, one Saturday evening, he failed to answer when called for dinner. I found him sitting at the old table that had come with us from San Justo, his cards spread before him in his accustomed solitaire, asleep, not to wake for us again, — a beautiful way to go, no pain, no days of helplessness.

This meant the breaking up of the home, for we young folk scattered, Nan to Wellesley to finish her interrupted course, Llewellyn to Pomona College where he had been during the fall, and I to make a new home in the East.

Since my marriage I have not lived actually in Los Angeles. For eight years, divided between Michigan, Chicago, Honolulu and Cambridge, Massachusetts, my home was outside of California; but even during that time I made several visits here so that in all my life from the first trip south from San Justo before I was a year old to the present, I have never been away from Los Angeles for a period longer than two years. Since my return to my own state, twenty-one years ago I have always been within hailing distance. I have seen a city increase and multiply in an amazing manner, even an hundredfold, a strange experience for one who has no intention of being old for a long time yet. Those who realize how this infant prodigy of a town is daily swamped with hordes of new and unrelated people have patience with some things for which she can be justly criticized; they take pride in the vigor of her life and have faith that when she really grows up and discovers a coordinated spirit to direct her overgrown body, she will earn a right to her queenly name.

It is because these vanished days are so clear to me that I have put down some of the things I know for those who care to read, among whom I hope will be found the thirty grandchildren of the Hathaway-Bixby couples who have figured in the narrative.

The older people who have come into my record are all gone except Aunt Margaret and Aunt Martha, both well beyond their threescore years and ten. They live in Long Beach, the new city on the old ranch barley fields.

I began my book with a dedication to my father. I close it with a loving greeting to my two aunts, the remaining "Hathaway girls;" the one who welcomed me into the world and has been to me always the soul of generosity and kindness, the other for more than forty years a devoted mother to me, a woman of culture and character, whose alert mind still follows the best thought of the day, and whose big heart spends itself for the welfare of the oppressed.

My aunts, I salute you.

INDEX

INDEX